INDOCHINA: PERSPECTIVES FOR RECONCILIATION

INDOCHINA: PERSPECTIVES FOR RECONCILIATION

Edited and with an Introduction by

Peter A. Poole

Ohio University
Center for International Studies
Papers in International Studies
Southeast Asia Series No. 36

PREFACE

With the signing of the cease-fire agreement on Vietnam in early 1973 and the subsequent withdrawal of American military forces from that country, a change has occurred in United States foreign policy which warrants the most careful scholarly attention and analysis. Even a cursory reading of the daily newspapers makes it clear that this nation is now and will continue to be intensely involved with that area, the differences being in direction and purpose rather than in the degree of that involvement. Therefore, the Center for International Studies welcomes the opportunity to publish these studies of the situation in Indochina in all its complexity.

The views of Zasloff and Brown, as presented in Part II, were originally set forth in an article in Asian Survey for February 1974, and have been slightly revised as they appear here. The remaining papers were originally prepared for presentation at the Association for Asian Studies meeting in Chicago on April 1, 1973, and have also been updated. A brief word about each of the authors makes clear their qualifications to discuss the problem:

Joseph J. Zasloff is professor of political science at the University of Pittsburgh, author of The Pathet Lao and co-author of Indochina in Conflict: A Political Assessment. His co-author on the present paper, MacAlister Brown, is an associate professor of political science at Williams College in Williamstown, Massachusetts.

Bernard K. Gordon, chairman of the political science department at the University of New Hampshire, has also authored Dimensions of Conflict in Southeast Asia and Toward Disengagement in Asia: A Strategy for American Foreign Policy.

Harold C. Hinton is professor of international relations at George Washington University, and the author of China's Turbulent Quest and Communist China in World Politics.

At the time of the writing of Part IV, Nguyen Tien Hung was an associate professor of economics at Howard University in Washington, D.C.,

and had served for a number of years with the International Monetary Fund.
He is currently Minister of Planning for the government of the Republic
of Vietnam.

Peter A. Poole, editor of the collection and author of Part V, is
chairman of Southeast Asian Area Studies for the Foreign Service Institute
of the Department of State. He has previously published The Vietnamese in
Thailand: A Historical Perspective and The United States and Indochina,
from FDR to Nixon. The Southeast Asia Series already includes another
papers of his, The Expansion of the Vietnam War into Cambodia: Action and
Response by the Governments of North Vietnam, South Vietnam, Cambodia, and
the United States (No. 17, 1970).

We are pleased to include this set of studies in our Southeast Asia
Series.

Paul W. van der Veur
Editor
Papers in International Studies,
    Southeast Asia Series

CONTENTS

I: INTRODUCTION

Peter A. Poole

The United States failed in its twenty-year struggle to shape the future of Indochina. Far too much reliance was placed on military force, and the political aims of people living in the region were virtually ignored. Having more or less accepted this judgment, many Americans simply wanted to bring all their troops home -- and to hear no more about Indochina. In early 1974, America's military disengagement seemed unlikely to be reversed, but the level of U.S. military aid to South Vietnam and Cambodia remained high, and American aims in these two countries had not been clarified. No one could say when peace would return to Cambodia or South Vietnam or even whether they would emerge from war as distinct political units.

However, in Laos, the prospects for political compromise were encouraging, as viewed by MacAlister Brown and Joseph Zasloff in Part II. Not only had a coalition government been formed, but a system of joint policing of Vientiane and Luang Prabang had begun by units loyal to the Pathet Lao and to the old Royal Lao Government. The long period of extremely cautious negotiation which led up to the formation of the new government in April 1974 had apparently served to build confidence gradually between the two sides.

The Laotian agreement called for the withdrawal of all foreign troops from Laos within sixty days after the formation of a coalition government. Professors Zasloff and Brown indicate that a likely move by Chinese and North Vietnamese troops in Laos may be to exchange their uniforms for mufti and become "technical assistance" personnel. They acknowledge, also, that any foreign troops that are withdrawn could be returned on a few days notice. However, the authors suggest that the actual removal of foreign troops, including Thai units and U.S. military advisors, would encourage the Lao to continue trying to settle their differences among themselves.

In analyzing the Indochina interests of Peking, Hanoi, and Moscow, Harold C. Hinton (in Part III) sees more basis for conflict than for cooperation. The global Sino-Soviet rivalry will cause friction between the two powers in Indochina (and other parts of the Third World) even if the element of direct confrontation diminishes. China and the Soviet Union will each try to maintain viable relations with North Vietnam, but they will each also continue, for the next few years, to place a higher priority on their relations with the United States. Thus, much will depend on the future relationship between Hanoi and Washington and the extent to which the United States maintains an active interest in the fate of Indochina.

Meanwhile, according to Professor Hinton, the long-standing, semi-suppressed rivalry between Peking and Hanoi for influence in Indochina -- and in North and Northeast Thailand -- is likely to continue, subject to the important priorities already mentioned. This suggests that the Soviet Union enjoys a certain advantage over China simply because it is not competing with Hanoi for regional influence. The Soviet Union's advantage can only be enhanced by its superior capacity for extending industrial aid. In short, Hanoi may find that the price it will have to pay in the future for actively pursuing its goal of regional domination will be a serious imbalance in its relations with Peking and Moscow.

In Part IV, Dr. Nguyen Thien Hung suggests that economic interests are among the most basic forces that motivate the North and South Vietnamese governments -- and that these interests would be served to a remarkable degree by reviving the old Indochinese Economic Union. Prior to partition in 1954, the area that is now the Democratic Republic of Vietnam depended heavily on the southern (Republic of Vietnam) area for food "imports." In return, the North provided a large percentage of the cement and coal which the South needed and lacked. Thus, there was a striking interdependence between North and South Vietnam before the rupture of economic ties in 1954, and during the past two decades the two regions have continued to import from other countries large quantities of products which they could have obtained from each other.

This inherent interdependence of the two regions, Dr. Hung believes, is a strong incentive for resuming trade under the German formula of "two zones in one economic entity". A revived Indochinese Economic Union would logically embrace Laos and Cambodia as well as North and South Vietnam. Much of the French-built infrastructure for economic exchange between the states of Indochina remains intact or could easily be replaced. To allow the people of all four countries to move about freely and to seek employment in any part of the Union would make for maximum economic efficiency.

In time, Dr. Hung believes, the effective functioning of an economic union might lead to further steps toward political integration of Indochina.

However, there are obvious political obstacles to such a union. As Peter A. Poole relates in Part V, both the Thai and Khmer governments officially regard the Vietnamese minorities in their countries as subversive and unassimilable. On the other hand, both governments have found that massive efforts at repatriating the Vietnamese residents have produced serious disadvantages for all concerned. Indeed, neither Thailand nor Cambodia can prevent quite large numbers of Vietnamese immigrants from filtering across their borders in search of economic or physical security. Adopting a hard-line approach toward these minority groups seems merely to invite retribution from Hanoi and perhaps Saigon.

There are signs that the Thai are beginning to test the historic dogma that Vietnamese are unassimilable; a relaxation of restrictive measures has been accompanied by evidence that the Vietnamese residents hope to be absorbed into Thai society. As for Cambodia, its future leaders seem likely to adopt a middle course in their policy toward Vietnam and the Vietnamese minority -- between the extreme policies that have been followed during the past decade, first by Sihanouk and then by Lon Nol.

In Part VI Bernard K. Gordon describes the mood of ambivalence and uncertainty in which both Japan and the United States seek to overcome their past failures in Indochina. Even among those who recognize that the circumstances of East Asia may now justify or even require new American and Japanese policies towards Indochina and Southeast Asia, no policy roads seem especially well-lighted. Rather, the emphasis is on presenting the smallest possible target to domestic critics or foreign adversaries.

American officials show little urgency about phasing out United States forces still in Thailand, even though most Americans regard with extreme distaste the prospect of their country becoming involved again in Southeast Asian hostilities. In late 1973, there were only the faintest indications that a new economic rationale might be sought for American involvement in Southeast Asia. On the other hand, Japan, the leading economic power in Southeast Asia, was slowly and painfully accepting the fact that a more visible political role was unavoidable.

The governments of both Japan and the United States were in a mood to welcome the strengthening of existing non-military regional organizations in Southeast Asia and perhaps to urge or support the creation of new ones. There seemed more likelihood of the United States and Japan playing a constructive role in this manner than by trying to persuade Peking and Moscow to accept the concept of a "quadrilateral balance of power" -- in which only the United States fully believed.

II: LAOS 1973; WARY STEPS TOWARD PEACE*

MacAlister Brown
and
Joseph J. Zasloff

Negotiating the Agreement

Negotiations between the Royal Lao Government (RLG) and the Pathet Lao (PL) for a cease-fire were underway seriously in Vientiane in the last months of 1972. The basis of discussion was an expanded version of the Five Points which the Pathet Lao originally announced in March 1970. Weekly sessions had begun on October 17, and made good progress even during the snags in the Paris Talks on Vietnam. Both sides produced draft peace agreements, differing principally on the method of reconstituting the government following a cease-fire. The Pathet Lao proposed that, pending general elections, a Coalition Council be appointed as a quasi-legislature, and a Provisional Government be formed on a tripartite basis of Pathet Lao, rightist, and the PL-allied "patriotic neutralist" factions. The Government insisted that the Pathet Lao either return to the existing tripartite government which they had abandoned in 1963, or join a new tripartite cabinet in which Premier Souvanna Phouma's followers would continue to be recognized as the neutralists.

The conclusion of the Paris Agreement and Protocols on Ending the War and Restoring Peace in Vietnam on January 23, 1973, cast a new light on the Laos situation. Article 20 of the Paris Agreement called upon the participating parties to abide by the 1962 Geneva Agreements on Laos and respect the Lao people's rights to independence, sovereignty, unity, territorial integrity, and neutrality. In his press conference after the Agreement, the chief American negotiator, Henry A. Kissinger, indicated that it was "clearly understood that North Vietnamese troops are considered foreign with respect to Laos and Cambodia." It was his "firm expectation that within a short period of time there will be a formal cease-fire in Laos which, in turn will lead to a withdrawal of all foreign forces from Laos

---

*This paper first appeared as an article in the February 1974 issue of Asian Survey. It has been slightly revised. It is included here with the permission of the original publisher, California University Press.

and, of course, to the end of the use of Laos as a corridor of infiltration." He specified that his confidence in this matter was based upon exchanges that had taken place which he could not elaborate, but that there
were no secret formal obligations.

Some of this confidence was shortly vindicated with the signing in
Vientiane, on February 21, 1973, of the Agreement on the Restoration of
Peace and Reconciliation in Laos. The Agreement retained most of the
flavor of the Pathet Lao's draft, both in its terminology ("Patriotic
Forces side" *versus* "Vientiane Government side") and its provisions. These
included scrupulous application of the 1962 Geneva Agreements, particularly
cessation of bombing and termination of foreign-supported "special forces"
and all other military activities by foreign countries and the Lao factions.
The Agreement also called for withdrawal of all foreign military personnel
and installations within sixty days of the establishment of the Provisional
Government and the National Coalition Council. Both sides were required to
return all prisoners, regardless of nationality, as well as those imprisoned for cooperating with the other side, within the same time period, and
then to gather and report information on those missing in action (which includes over 300 Americans).

The political arrangements followed the Pathet Lao draft for the most
part, but the details remained to be set down in a protocol. Within thirty
days of the Agreement (a deadline far too short for so delicate an opera-
tion), a Provisional Government of National Union (PGNU) and a National
Coalition Political Council (NCPC) were to be formed under special proced-
ures utilizing the King. Pending elections to be arranged, "both sides
will preserve their own zones of temporary control" (a *de facto* administrative partition), but promote normal relations of travel and economic exchange.

Thus a framework for national peace and political accommodation was
agreed upon, but negotiation of a protocol and its implementation would
require much more mutual trust. The Pathet Lao had given up their previous
insistence on a political settlement before a military cease-fire, and they
had not specifically abolished the National Assembly (rather they rendered
it redundant), nor loaded the provisional government in their favor. Nevertheless, the Agreement left them jubilant.

Maneuvering Toward the Protocol

In the negotiation of the Protocol to the peace agreement, Prime Minister Souvanna Phouma believed that the PL's commitment to Lao nationalism was stronger than the ties to their North Vietnamese allies, or to Marxism-Leninism, and that they could be drawn back into the Lao community. The PL, negotiating from a stronger military and political position than in 1962, were ready for an accommodation which would speed the American departure and bring them into a government in which they would control half of the ministries, participate in administration of the RLG zone, and acquire a legitimate presence in the administrative and royal capitals of the country. Both sides were encouraged to reach a compromise by the U.S. and North Vietnam, as well as by the other Great Powers. For example, toward the end of the negotiations the Soviet military attaché, after consultation with his U.S. counterpart, gave a dinner party with vodka to ease tensions between PL and RLG generals.

Within his own community Souvanna met opposition, particularly from right-wing army officers and powerful political families such as the Sananikones. In late August the oft-predicted coup was attempted by Thao Ma, a former Royal Lao Air Force chief of staff living in Thailand since his earlier abortive coup attempt in 1966, with a small band of perhaps twenty co-conspirators. They apparently expected to be joined by Air Force and other FAR (Forces Armies Royales) officers disaffected by Souvanna's moves toward accommodation. U.S. Chargé d'Affaires John Dean plunged rapidly into the fray at the Vientiane airfield, attempting to persuade Ma (who in earlier years had enjoyed abundant American support) to abandon his scheme. Unsuccessful in this effort, Dean vigorously advised FAR officers not to support the coup. It died within a day, with Thao Ma and several leaders summarily shot by Army officers, leaving a mystery as to whether other Lao rightists or Thais had helped plan the effort. Paradoxically, the coup bolstered the weary Souvanna's position, as the reluctant FAR and the entire diplomatic community expressed support for his personal role. The cabinet opposition which had blocked an accord in July was now gradually isolated and exhausted, and Souvanna arranged the official signing ceremony for September 14, 1973.

PL spokesmen have hailed it as a "great victory for the Lao people". The Protocol includes the following provisions:

1. A Premier (whom all agreed would be Souvanna) is to head a government composed of a Vice Premier and five ministers from each side and two more ministers chosen by mutual consent. Each minister will have a vice-minister from the other side with whom he must work on a basis of unanimity.

2. The PGNU is to function on all important matters by unanimity. However, each party is responsible for the ministries under its charge, and even a minister's temporary absence is to be filled by his own party, rather than by the other party's vice minister.

3. The NCPC, composed of 42 members (16 from each side plus 10 more chosen by common agreement), will be chaired by a PL member and will operate on the principle of unanimity. It will meet once every six months (for not more than one month), functioning between sessions through an equally balanced Standing Committee.

4. The PGNU and NCPC are "two independent and equal organs . . .cooperating in the handling of state affairs, under . . . the king." (The Council will share in preparing for general elections "as soon as possible", but otherwise its role seems less than equal. If the PGNU should not agree with the Council's recommendations, the PGNU must simply give clear and "sufficient" explanations.)

5. Each side will contribute an equal number of troops for security duties and personnel for a joint police force to insure neutralization of Vientiane and Luang Prabang. All other armed forces must withdraw under the direction of the Central Joint Commission for the Implementation of the Agreement (CJCIA).

6. The CJCIA, composed of 7 members from each side, will operate, with small joint mobile teams, in close collaboration with the ICC, which will supervise withdrawal of foreign troops and investigate cease-fire violations by foreign forces. Twenty-seven cease-fire landmarks will be designated, and in a few places the CJCIA may position troops of one side in areas controlled by the other.

7. Refugees may choose freely to remain or return to their native villages, and should be assisted.

The Pathet Lao's demands were thwarted to the extent that refugees are not *required* to return to their villages, cease-fire markers do not constitute an undeviating line of demarcation and some government officials are authorized to travel freely in either zone. The Pathet Lao's deputy premier is not unique or superior to the other side's and, contrary to PL wishes, the date of general elections was not fixed.

In sum, the Protocol builds logically on the Agreement, even though the chances of the political mechanism ever moving out of the garage remain problematical. The two documents are replete with safeguards against submission to the preferences of merely one party, and a western democrat can easily scoff at their requirements of unanimity. The PL has moved from a representation of two ministers in 1957 to one-third of the ministries (including a vice-premier) in 1962, to one-half of the ministries and vice-ministries (including a vice-premier) in 1973. The territory "temporarily" under their control now comprises three-fourths of the country, and elements of their forces are stationed in the "neutralized" capital cities. On the other hand, an explicit partition has been avoided and there has been progress toward national concord.

The Military Picture, 1973

The movement toward an agreement in both Vietnam and Laos prompted increased hostilities in Laos in late 1972 and early 1973. Both sides, encouraged and supported by their external allies, the U.S. and North Vietnam, sought to secure control of territory and people before a cease-fire, as well as to apply military pressure on the negotiators. The Pathet Lao emerged from the cease-fire in 1973 with distinct gains in territory over the position they had achieved in 1962. The PL now controlled about three-fourths of the total land area, although less than half of the population, and principally hill tribes, while the RLG dominated the Mekong River valley areas populated largely by lowland Lao.

Shortly after the cease-fire, military activity flared again as both sides moved in selected areas to consolidate positions and to establish clearly discernible demarcation lines. Two engagements during this series appeared especially serious, one at Pak Song on the Bolovens Plateau in south Laos in late February and another at Tha Vieng, just south of the Plain of Jars, in mid-April. The U.S. renewed bombing raids against these sites, and spokesmen for President Nixon, despite heavy criticism within Congress, warned that the U.S. would continue to respond positively to RLG requests for air strikes if such major violations continued. Despite violent charges and counter-charges on both sides, the hostilities abated with only minor local adjustments in territorial control. Although both sides maintained their forces in place, by the end of the year, contrasted with South Vietnam and Cambodia, the cease-fire was holding well.

The following table shows the military strength of the two sides, as estimated by U.S. government sources, shortly following the cease-fire and at the end of the year.

MILITARY FORCES IN LAOS[1]
(according to U.S. Government estimates)

	March 31, 1973	December 1973
Royal Lao Government Side[2]		
Royal Lao Army (Forces Armees Royales, FAR):		
Infantry	38,500	
Air Force	2,050	
River Flotilla	330	
Irregulars	18,000[3]	
Other		
Neutralists	5,800	
	68,180	60,000
Thai Irregulars	17,330	5-7,000
	(27 Infantry Battalions, 3 Artillery Battalions)	(approx. 10 Battalions)
Communist Forces[4]		
Pathet Lao		
In North Laos	24,000	
In South Laos	11,000	
	35,000	30-40,000 (includes Patriotic Neutralists)
Patriotic Neutralists		
All in North Laos	2,000	
North Vietnamese		
In North Laos	10,000	
In South Laos	60,000	
	(including 55,000 supply, transport, and defense forces along the Ho Chi Minh Trail)	
	70,000	55-70,000 (includes at least 50% assigned to Ho Chi Minh Trail)
Chinese Road Project		
Chinese Forces	30,000	10-20,000 or 30,000[5]

[1]Principal sources:

    1. Interviews by the authors with U.S. government officials in Washington in April, September, and December 1973.

    2. *Thailand, Laos, Cambodia, and Vietnam: April 1973*. A Staff Report Prepared for the Use of the Subcommittee on U.S. Security Agreements and Commitments Abroad of the Committee on Foreign Relations, U.S. Senate,

As for the U.S. military presence in Laos, in early April there were plans to phase out the CIA paramilitary advisors and support personnel and to scale down U.S. Army and Air Force advisors, to reduce the Requirements Office (which administers U.S. military assistance in Laos) and to terminate the Air America contract. Although some of these reductions took place (both as a token of good faith and as economy measures), full implementation of these plans will await North Vietnamese performance in keeping the Laos agreements.[6] The U.S.-supported Thai irregulars have apparently been reduced to 10 battalions by the end of the year, and officials in Washington indicate that the U.S. will continue to support these forces until the disposition of the North Vietnamese forces within Laos becomes clear. Since the cease-fire and protocol called for the withdrawal of all foreign forces "within 60 days at the latest" after the formation of the PGNU, both sides are apparently bargaining for the withdrawal of their adversary's foreign troop support by retaining some foreign troops on their own side.

Implementing the Protocol

The most important sign that accommodation was taking place at the end of 1973 was the arrival of PL troops in the capitals, about 1500 airlifted by the Soviet Union to Vientiane and about 1,000 by the Chinese People's Republic to Luang Prabang. Souvanna Phouma had personally pushed ahead with the airlifts soon after the signing of the Protocol, but more cautious

---

June 11, 1973. This report was prepared by James G. Lowenstein and Richard M. Moose. As staff members of the Senate Foreign Relations Committee, they were given official U.S. government estimates by the U.S. Mission in Vientiane and by officials of the executive branch in Washington. This report will hereafter be referred to as the Lowenstein-Moose Report.

[2] These figures, provided to Lowenstein and Moose, were general estimates by the U.S. Army Attaché's office which advises that they may be inflated by as much as 10%.

[3] These irregulars were formally integrated into the FAR on Feb. 20, 1973.

[4] An alternate set of estimates given to Lowenstein and Moose for the March 1973 period showed totals of 27,760 PL, 1,725 Neutralists, and 61,610 North Vietnamese troops in Laos.

[5] One U.S. Government agency cited 10-20,000 Chinese troops; another retained the 30,000 figure.

[6] Lowenstein-Moose Report, p. 17. The total U.S. mission in Laos was reported to be 1,174 as of February 1, 1973.

elements within the FAR brought suspension of the flights in mid-October until the CJCIA was organized and prepared to regulate arrival of military equipment. The flights resumed after several weeks delay and by the year's end, PL troops were practically all at their new stations. The local populations have accepted the newcomers, who live much to themselves, with equanimity and customary Lao goodwill, and the newly-arrived "country boys" ogle the big city.

Prospects are good that the new government will be formed some time in 1974. The Pathet Lao, recalling the threats to their leaders and the military coups of the 1960s in Vientiane, have insisted first upon the full neutralization of the two capitals. The FAR are constructing a base outside Vientiane, unlikely to be completed before the spring of 1974, to which their troops (not assigned to Vientiane or Luang Prabang) are to be moved. Membership of the PGNU has not been announced, but informed speculation brings forth the following probabilities:

Premier -- Prince Souvanna Phouma (incumbent)

From the Vientiane Side	From the PL Side
Vice Premier: Leum Insisienmay, current Minister of Information, rightist	Vice Premier: Prince Souphanouvong, half brother of Souvanna Phouma, Deputy Premier in 1962 Tripartite Government
Defense: Sisouk Na Champassack, current Minister of Finance and acting Minister of Defense, rightist	Foreign Ministry: Prince Souphanouvong or Phoumi Vongvichit
Finance: Ngon Sananikone, current Minister of Public Works, neutralist	Economy and Planning: Khamsouk Keola, neutralist aligned with PL; or Prince Souphanouvong
Interior: Pheng Phongsavan, incumbent, neutralist	Information: Phoumi Vongvichit or Khamsouk Keola
Health: Khamphay Abhay, former Minister of Health, rightist; or Prince Sisoumang, nephew of King Savang Vatthana	Religion: Maha Kou Souvannamethi or Maha Khampha, both neutralists aligned with the PL
Education: Leum Insisienmay	Public Works: Prince Souk Vongsak

For the two Ministries of Post, Telephone, and Telegraph, and of Justice, to which personalities agreeable to both sides are to be appointed, Tay Keolongkut, a former Minister of Health, has been mentioned as the RLG candidate, but the PL candidate remains undisclosed. For Chairman of the NCPC, the PL are expected to appoint Nouhak Phongsavan.

Pending the general elections, a loss of Souvanna Phouma, who has been indispensable to the compromise, could prove fatal. The Protocol does not give the post of Premier to either party and requires cabinet unanimity, but customarily in Laos the principle of age prevails, which would give 64-year-old Souphanouvong the presumption over Leum Insisienmay, and might preserve the fabric of the coalition.

The Protocol's stipulation that elections be held "as soon as possible" seems unlikely to be fulfilled until there is a clearer resolution of the struggle for power. Elections seem destined to serve more as a process to ratify conditions which have been accepted by the leaders rather than as a contest to determine who will rule. The RLG seem the least likely to press for early elections. Members of the RLG National Assembly are unlikely to favor an election which will retire them from office prior to the expiration of their mandate in 1977. Moreover, RLG leaders are fearful of electoral competition with the PL who possess, unlike the RLG, cohesive leadership, a unified party and front, zealous cadres, and a doctrine of political mobilization.

The notion of ministries jointly administered by political enemies may seem impossible to the Western mind, but it is not inconceivable in Laos. It appears likely that each party will dominate its own ministries, and do its best to block inimical actions in the other's, with a result that only the most consensual activities will be possible at the national level. To the extent that Laos can remove itself from the arena of Great Power contention and can insulate itself from the struggle for control of Vietnam, this low level of national administrative initiative might permit a measure of stability in a localized and economically undeveloped society. Whether administrative integration of the country can grow through gradual extension of governmental services, such as post and telegraph, roads, or public health on a nation-wide basis remains very much in doubt. Yet this remains the gleam in the eye of Laotians who care about national unity first and remain open-minded about socialism as a political creed for their country.

The major social issue facing the new government will be to deal with the 370,000 current refugees, and perhaps an equal number of people who have settled in RLG territory. The economic problems raised by their return or resettlement will be burdensome, and both sides will vie to control them, since their numbers are politically important.

Even a more stable peace is unlikely to alter Laos's heavy dependency on external aid to maintain solvency. Assuming that military expenditures

(now about 50% of the RLG budget) can be reduced, and the resultant infla-
tionary pressures subside (RLG prices rose approximately 30% in 1973), it
is possible that aid could be shifted from budgetary support to development.
The chief instrument for controlling inflation since 1964 has been the Foreign Exchange Operations Fund (FEOF) to which donor countries (the princi-
pal one being the United States) make contributions of foreign exchange.
PL officials have spoken favorably about the continuation of FEOF, and it
is likely that they would wish for aid from the United States and other
Western countries. Whether the conditions for the granting of aid will be
politically suitable to both parties in Laos, as well as to the donor
countries, particularly the U.S., remains an important question.

The road network under construction by the Chinese in Northwest Laos
was expanded during 1973, and work is likely to continue throughout 1974.
Once the 60-day deadline for foreign troop exit begins, with the formation
of the PGNU and NCPC, it would not be surprising to learn that the Chinese
troops engaged in the construction and security tasks had exchanged their
uniforms for mufti and were designated members of a technical assistance
mission. The North Vietnamese might adopt a similar strategy for their
personnel servicing the Ho Chi Minh Trail in south Laos.

Since the cease-fire, the North Vietnamese have been vigorously expan-
ding the Ho Chi Minh Trail system. In addition, they have rapidly developed another road network within South Vietnam which pierces the DMZ and
moves south through the central highlands. This second system, with a different rainfall season than the first, has, according to U.S. and South
Vietnamese sources, contributed significantly to heavy infiltration of personnel and supplies from the north during the past year. Since the area in
southern Laos is sparsely populated by hill tribes, RLG officials have continued their tacit policy of regarding the Trail's use to be the problem of
the South Vietnamese and the U.S., recognizing that they have little ability, in any case, to alter the situation. U.S. spokesmen object publicly to
the North Vietnamese violation of Lao territory, but with U.S. forces out
of Vietnam, there is little now that the U.S. is willing to do to restrict
North Vietnamese use. Despite the Protocol's prohibition on "espionage by
air and ground means", the U.S. continues its reconnaissance flights over
Lao territory to monitor the other side and register its own continuing
position in the military contest.

As for unresolved military issues, withdrawal of the remaining North Vietnamese and Thai troops and American military advisors from Laos, in compliance with the Agreement's stipulations, would provide strong reinforcement to the wary steps toward concord in Laos. Although it is true that troops could be reintroduced in a matter of days, particularly from neighboring North Vietnam and Thailand, their withdrawal would have an important symbolic effect, further encouraging the Lao to settle their differences among themselves. The PL are likely to continue voicing their objection to the integration of the Lao irregulars into the FAR, but if the U.S. terminates its special relationship with these irregulars, the issue is not likely to be of critical importance. In fact both a stable peace and political reconciliation depend upon the willingness of the external powers to disengage from their injurious intrusion in Laos.

III: CHINESE AND SOVIET INTERESTS IN INDOCHINA

Harold C. Hinton

A number of assumptions can reasonably be made about Indochina following the signing of the 1973 agreements. One is that there will be "reconciliation by firing squad", or in other words a continuation, at a level
of violence just low enough not to bring back the B-52s, of the Vietnamese
Communist movement's generation-old struggle to unify Vietnam under its
own domination and to control the rest of Indochina through its allies or
proxies. Another is that the Sino-Soviet dispute will remain active, in
the sense that fairly acute rivalry in third areas, including Indochina,
will persist, even if the level of direct confrontation between Peking and
Moscow declines.

Common or Parallel Sino-Soviet Interests in Indochina

This is a story quickly told. Neither party to the Sino-Soviet dispute wants a major escalation of the Indochina war (and in all probability
neither has ever wanted one), on the ground that it would be directly or
indirectly dangerous to itself and might benefit the other. On the other
hand, each party has continued for largely political reasons (including its
rivalry with the other) to supply Hanoi with variable amounts of military
as well as economic aid.

For at least as long as the United States continues to be significantly involved in Indochina, neither party to the Sino-Soviet dispute wants
to see a defeat for North Vietnam (because it might get the blame) or a
clearcut victory (if only because the other might get the credit). Nor
does either adversary very much want further American military withdrawals
from the region, because they might create a situation advantageous to the
other.

Finally, and most important of all, each party to the Sino-Soviet dispute regards its generally improving relationship with the United States as
more valuable, precisely on account of the existence of the dispute to a
large extent, than its rather troublesome relationship with North Vietnam,
even though the latter cannot be jeopardized to the point where Hanoi moves
into the arms of the adversary. An excellent illustration of the importance of the United States to the two adversaries in the Vietnamese context

is that Moscow did not, and indeed was in no position to, cancel the summit meeting of May 1972 on account of the American bombing of North Vietnam and the mining of Haiphong.

Peking and Indochina

Inasmuch as Indochina borders on southern China, Peking inevitably views the region from the perspective of its own security. In this connection it is virtually essential that North Vietnam remain at least formally friendly to Peking, even though for a variety of reasons, including the provisions of the 1954 Geneva agreements, there is no treaty of alliance between North Vietnam and China (or between North Vietnam and the Soviet Union). Similarly, Peking has effectively created a buffer zone-*cum*-sphere of influence for itself in northwestern Laos, to the virtual exclusion of Hanoi and any one else (including the Royal Laotian Government). Its main probable purposes include the prevention of an American, Thai, or North Vietnamese presence in that area. As already indicated, Peking has sought to avoid a confrontation with the United States over Indochina and has therefore discouraged Hanoi from escalating the war in the south above the level of "people's war", although of course not always successfully.

The matter of Peking's quest for influence in Indochina is rather more complex, partly because it includes an effort to prevent the Soviet Union from increasing its own influence. One of Peking's reasons for objecting to escalation of the war has probably been that it tends to drive Hanoi closer to Moscow in search of heavy weapons, which since 1965 have generally been forthcoming. Because of its reluctance to become involved in a confrontation with the United States, Peking has not attempted to provide North Vietnam with actual protection, except indirectly through playing on the American fear of another war with China, but it has furnished Hanoi not only with moral, political, and propaganda support but also with arms and grain. The weapons that Peking has furnished Hanoi have been for the most part infantry weapons, or in other words, weapons not particularly suitable to major offensive operations.

It is reasonably clear, especially if one uses the comparatively enthusiastic Chinese position on Korean unification as a standard of comparison, that Peking is not genuinely in favor of the unification of Vietnam under Hanoi's control, or of North Vietnamese domination of the rest of

Indochina. The reason is simple: Hanoi is already a troublesome partner for Peking in some respects, and if it controlled the whole of Indochina it would be a serious rival in Mainland Southeast Asia. One reason for Peking's lack of enthusiasm for military escalation in Indochina has probably been its potential for moving Hanoi closer to such a position of dominance. As is suggested by its playing host, apparently at Canton, to the "summit conference of the Indochinese peoples" (April 1970), Peking evidently would like to provide the main link among, and at least a degree of guidance for, the four main leftist states or movements in Indochina: North Vietnam, the National Liberation Front and the Provisional Revolutionary Government of South Vietnam, Prince Sihanouk and his heterogeneous coalition, and the Pathet Lao. But Hanoi's influence on the other components of this group tends to exceed that of Peking, whose standing in their eyes has been compromised at least to a degree by the obvious priority it places on its new relationship with the United States.

For the main current trend in Chinese foreign policy is not to appear as a promoter of Hanoi's interests by urging it to fight on against American "imperialism", as was the tendency until recently, but rather to seek gradual accommodation with the United States mainly in order to balance Soviet pressures on the Sino-Soviet border and Soviet competition with China elsewhere, including Indochina. The People's Republic of China wants an American military withdrawal from Taiwan, as long as it does not lead to a growth of Soviet influence in Taipei, and accordingly the United States promised in the Shanghai Communiqué of February 1972 to withdraw its remaining military personnel from Taiwan, where they are largely involved in logistical support for the American military presence in Indochina and Thailand, "as the tension in the area diminishes." Peking appears to regard this pledge as an additional incentive for its own good behavior toward the trouble spots of the region: Korea, the Taiwan Strait, and Indochina. It is possible that Peking successfully opposed a 1972 Tet offensive by the North Vietnamese, if only because it would have begun inconveniently close to the Nixon visit to China. Peking was not very difficult about the American bombing and mining operations commencing on May 8, 1972, following the North Vietnamese invasion of South Vietnam that had begun on March 30, or about American bombing of North Vietnam in December 1972 or of parts of Cambodia down to August 15, 1973. Peking increased the level

extent of direct military involvement, has been the need it felt to compete with Peking for influence on Hanoi and indeed on all the other participants in the struggle. Moscow has been concerned to inflict a setback on the United States, mainly through Hanoi as its proxy; there are obvious analogies to this policy at other times and places, such as Korea in the early 1950's and the Middle East in recent years. Moscow has received considerable unwitting help from the wounds that the United States has inflicted upon itself through its overmilitarized conduct of its role in the struggle in Indochina. Soviet objectives have apparently included an essentially political, rather than military, takeover of the whole of Indochina by Hanoi, directly or by proxy, an outcome that Moscow has considered was being retarded rather than hastened by Hanoi's recurrent tendency toward escalation. Accordingly, since at least as long ago as 1965 the Soviet Union, while turning an uncooperative face toward the United States, has been applying quiet political pressure upon Hanoi with the aim of moving it toward a political settlement somewhat more rapidly than Hanoi appeared willing to move spontaneously. It was only in late 1972, however, when they were supplemented by parallel Chinese efforts and reinforced by the failure of the North Vietnamese Easter offensive, that these Soviet pressures became effective.

Despite its preference for a political approach on Hanoi's part, Moscow has found perhaps its main means of influence on the situation to be the supplying of arms to Hanoi, especially air defense equipment and heavy ground force weapons (tanks, artillery, etc.). The latter were particularly in evidence at the time of the North Vietnamese Easter offensive of 1972. The Soviet Union has faced the classic dilemma of all suppliers of arms to bellicose junior partners: how to acquire influence over the partner by providing the arms and yet to restrain him from using the arms in ways embarrassing or even dangerous to the supplier. The only solution to this problem appears to be to penetrate the recipient's military establishment with one's own advisers, but this approach conveys the obvious risk of a political clash in which the recipient of the arms holds the high cards, at least in the short run, as in the cases of China in 1927 and Egypt in 1972.

Since about 1971, Moscow's anti-American motivation with respect to Indochina has been significantly altered. Hanoi must still be wooed and supported at least to the minimum extent necessary to prevent it from throwing itself into Peking's arms, but a far more important consideration is the need to prevent the United States from doing the same. More precisely, the Soviet Union has become greatly concerned over the rapid development of a Sino-American accommodation and has become anxious to improve its own relations with the United States not only to counter this trend but to promote détente in Europe (a major purpose of which, in Moscow's eyes, may be to enable it to devote more attention to coping with Peking) and to bandage the limping Soviet economy through expanded trade and technological contacts with the United States and other developed countries. It was presumably with these considerations in mind that the Soviet leadership decided not to disrupt the Moscow summit on account of the American bombing and mining campaign in Vietnam, which had begun two weeks earlier (on May 8, 1972).

Vietnam and the Sino-Soviet-American Triangle

There is no question that Hanoi, whose main objective appears to be overthrowing the Saigon government and ultimately reuniting Vietnam, regarded both the Sino-Soviet border confrontation of 1969 and the improvement of each adversary's relations with the United States since about 1971 as major setbacks to the achievement of that objective and has been correspondingly angered at both Peking and Moscow. As between the two, its anger at Moscow appears to be the less, or at least the better controlled, probably because of its long-standing rivalry with Peking, the Soviet Union's superior capacity to provide aid, and the fact that Moscow still has custody of the symbols of pre-eminent legitimacy in the international communist movement.

As might be expected, Peking has tried to soothe North Vietnamese feelings by steps falling short of major substantive concessions. Chou En-lai flew secretly to Hanoi early in March 1972, probably to convey assurances that no deals on Vietnam had been made at the Peking summit. But the Chinese did not allow their developing relationship with the United States to be jeopardized by more than propaganda protests and a limited increase in the flow of military aid to North Vietnam during the American bombing and mining campaign in the spring and summer of 1972. In fact, Peking appears to have been none too happy about the Easter offensive, to which the American campaign was a response. Soon afterward, according to a high official American source, general Chinese reservations about Hanoi, and particularly about its ambitions for effective control over the whole of Indochina, led Peking to threaten privately, and perhaps to implement, a reduction in the level of its military aid to North Vietnam as a means of encouraging the signing of an agreement. It is likely, then, that Chinese influence was an important, if not necessarily decisive, factor in producing the agreement of January 27, 1973.

This behavior came all the more naturally to Peking because of an evident irritation with Hanoi over its continuing close relations with Moscow. A delegation led by Truong Chinh encountered a rather cool reception in Peking in December 1972, very likely because its main mission was to visit Moscow on the occasion of the fiftieth anniversary of the founding of the Soviet Union, and furthermore at a time when North Vietnamese (as well as South Vietnamese) stubbornness had produced a temporary breakdown of the Paris negotiations and a resumption of the American bombing of North Vietnam.

Chinese treatment of North Vietnamese delegations became markedly more cordial after the signing of the agreement of January 27, 1973. Le Duc Tho was welcomed by Mao Tse-tung in person on his way home after the signing of the agreement. First Secretary Le Duan and Premier Pham Van Dong, when visiting Peking in early June 1973, were able to reach an agreement in which the Chinese promised to provide "gratuitous" economic aid. This apparently did not include military aid, and there are some indications that Peking privately took the United States-North Vietnamese agreement of June 13, 1973 (sometimes known as "Son of Ceasefire"), and the announcement at the end of June that the United States would stop bombing Cambodia on August 15 as a welcome pretext for reducing its military aid to North Vietnam and for encouraging Hanoi to do the same with respect to the Communist forces in Laos and Cambodia.

In general, Chinese propaganda has not echoed North Vietnamese charges that the United States has been violating the Vietnam ceasefire but has confined itself to assertions that Saigon is doing so and that the United States ought to enforce Saigon's compliance, as Peking seems to be implying it is doing with North Vietnam. Peking appears to be encouraging Hanoi's current tendency to build up, through economic aid and political support, the Provisional Revolutionary Government of South Vietnam in what is sometimes called the Third Vietnam (*i.e.*, the western portion of South Vietnam, including the highlands). It is worth repeating that it is important for Peking not to push Hanoi too far, so far for example that it draws significantly closer to Moscow. An additional and far more speculative point is that one reason for Peking's reluctance to alienate Hanoi may be a desire to keep open the possibility of calling on its good offices in the future to mediate the Sino-Soviet dispute.

Recent Soviet policy toward Vietnam has been essentially parallel, although of course competitive, with Peking's. As generally in the past, Moscow also clearly prefers a basically political to a largely military strategy on Hanoi's part and has apparently been restricting its military aid to North Vietnam since the January 27, 1973, agreement and still more since the June 13, 1973, agreement. Moscow also generally refrains from echoing Hanoi's charges that the United States has been violating the ceasefire. On the other hand, Moscow no more than Peking is in a position to allow its relations with Hanoi to deteriorate beyond the point of no return. One probable reason is that the Soviet Union presumably wants to include North Vietnam in any "collective security" system that it may be able to coax into existence in Asia; another is of course the likelihood that Peking would benefit from a worsening of Soviet-North Vietnamese relations. Evidence that Moscow has some sense of commitment to Hanoi is provided by a Soviet undertaking, given while Le Duan and Pham Van Dong were in Moscow in July 1973, to provide further economic aid and to make no charge for aid given during the war, which the Soviet leadership officially considers to be over.

Laos and Cambodia

Peking has pushed its so-called China Road through northwestern Laos to the Mekong River and appears to be using it, among other things, to train and supply actual and potential Thai and Meo guerrillas for action in Thailand. Of greater importance than this, however, at least in the Indochinese context, is the general diplomatic lineup in the negotiations leading to the Laos agreements of February 20, 1973, and subsequently. In effect, Peking supported the United States and the Royal Laotian Government (largely behind the scenes, of course) while Moscow sided more openly with North Vietnam and the Pathet Lao. Since the two Laotian adversaries were obviously moving, or were being pushed, toward an agreement, neither Moscow nor Peking needed to worry seriously that its own policy or its rivalry with its adversary might lead to an unwanted re-escalation of the war.

The Cambodian situation is more complicated, if only because no agreement has yet (April 1974) been reached between the contending parties and because Moscow and Peking maintain diplomatic relations with opposite sides.

It is fairly clear that North Vietnam has considerable direct contact with, and is in a position to exert influence on, the revolutionary coalition (the Cambodian National United Front, or FUNK) in Cambodia itself. China, on the other hand, must work largely through Prince Sihanouk, whom it has allowed to reside in Peking since his overthrow in March 1970 and whom it recognized in effect as the head of a government-in-exile on May 5 of that year. Sihanouk's influence on the FUNK, or at least on its operations in Cambodia, is questionable to say the least, although his diplomatic bargaining position appears to be improving as the major powers have failed to reach agreement on Cambodia as they have (nominally at least) on Vietnam and Laos. Cambodia has accordingly become a major agenda item, if not a serious issue, between Peking and Washington; Peking is limited to some extent by Sihanouk's views, which include strongly expressed opposition to negotiations with the United States and to any sort of partition of his country. As might be expected, Paking has been less critical of American Cambodian policy, at least in public, than Hanoi and Sihanouk have been. The United States-North Vietnamese agreement of June 13, 1973, and the cessation of American bombing on August 15, 1973, appear to have led to a reduction of Chinese military aid to the FUNK (mainly *via* North Vietnam), and possibly of Chinese political and diplomatic support for Sihanouk.

Moscow maintained diplomatic relations with the Lon Nol government until the fall of 1973, largely because of its intense dislike for the pro-Chinese Sihanouk. After experimenting, without visible success, with the idea of trying to encourage the formation of a legal Communist Party in Cambodia and to secure its admission into a coalition government in Phnom Penh, Moscow began in August 1973 to refer publicly to the FUNK as the "true representative of the people" of Cambodia, without mentioning Sihanouk in that connection. There were signs that Moscow was trying to promote a ceasefire and a coalition government analogous to those agreed on in Laos. After the non-aligned nations conference in Algeria adopted a pro-Sihanouk position, the Soviet Union granted something close to *de facto* recognition to Sihanouk's regime early in October 1973, probably in order to avoid diplomatic isolation in the event that Sihanouk's representatives were given Cambodia's U.N. seat.

Peking, Moscow, and the Future of Indochina

As along as the Sino-Soviet dispute persists at anything like its present level of bitterness -- and there is no convincing present evidence that a *rapprochement* is imminent; as long as each of the adversaries has better relations with the United States than it has with the other; and as long as the United States is regarded by each adversary as an important source of grain and high technology imports and as a still significant factor in Indochina, Peking and Moscow are likely to continue to value their relationship with the United States above their relationship with North Vietnam. For reasons already indicated, however, Hanoi can be ignored by neither. It is likely to continue to receive both outward political support and arms from both, accompanied by not necessarily effective injunctions against injecting the latter into South Vietnam, except at replacement levels as permitted by the agreement of January 27, 1973.

Beyond that, Soviet and Chinese Indochinese interests and policies can be expected to diverge significantly, as they have in the past.

Moscow is likely to view Indochina primarily from the perspective of its anti-Chinese strategy. This implies support for a level of agreement between Washington and Hanoi sufficient to permit the United States to pursue an orderly and gradual disengagement from the region, to Hanoi's advantage, without creating tempting opportunities that Peking might exploit; one means toward the latter end might be a serious Soviet effort to enroll Hanoi in a "collective security" system of some kind. Certainly the behavior to date of the Polish and Hungarian members of the International Commission of Control and Supervision for South Vietnam, which may be assumed to reflect the Soviet attitude, has been marked by a decided "tilt" in favor of Hanoi and the National Liberation Front.

Peking also favors, and will probably continue to favor, a political rather than a military solution to the Indochina question, one of a kind that would encourage the United States to withdraw its remaining personnel from Taiwan, would keep the Indochina states separate (although ideally all Communist-controlled and under at least a degree of Chinese influence), would restrain Hanoi without driving it into Moscow's arms, and would help to limit Soviet influence in the region. This appears to be a more complicated game than Moscow's, and one with a greater degree of parallelism with American policy than the Soviet game displays -- as long as Peking does not overplay its fairly weak (in the short run, at least) hand by some such ploy as an overly energetic effort to exploit Sihanouk as a handle on the Cambodian situation.

In the middle term, much may depend not only on Hanoi's rate of progress toward the achievement of its objectives but on the relative influence of the United States and the Soviet Union in the Indochina region. If the United States remains active and influential (not necessarily in a military sense) and maintains a reasonably viable relationship with Peking, China's chances for exercising significant influence in the region appear good. Otherwise, Soviet prospects look comparatively bright.

IV. PROSPECTS FOR ECONOMIC COOPERATION BETWEEN THE TWO VIETNAMS:
Implications for Indochina's Future

Nguyen Tien Hung

Article 15(c) of the January 23, 1973, Paris Cease-Fire Agreement on Vietnam stipulates:

> North and South Vietnam shall promptly start negotiations with a view to re-establishing normal relations in various fields. Among the questions to be negotiated are the modalities of civilian movement across the provisional military demarcation line.[1]

Article 10(b) of the February 22, 1973, Vientiane Accord on Laos declared:

> The two parties will initiate the carrying out of normal relations between the two governments, create favorable conditions which permit the people to move about, to seek the means of livelihood, to visit each other, to carry out economic cultural and other exchanges with a view to consolidating national union in order to rapidly fulfill the unification of the country.[2]

One can safely speculate that the cease-fire accord on Cambodia, once signed, will contain much the same provision for future negotiations between the two contending forces on the question of resuming normal relations among the people under their control.

Moreover, it seems clear that of all the possible "normal relations" among the states of Indochina, economic interchange is attractive enough to receive prompt attention from all parties concerned. How the Indochina partners move toward resuming their traditional economic links will certainly be a major topic of discussion in the years ahead when the time comes for negotiations on questions related to Articles 15(c) and 10(b) of the two agreements just mentioned.

This paper discusses the prospects for the resumption of economic relations between the two Vietnams during the post-cease-fire period and examines the effect of such a relationship on the future of all Indochina.

Because of the dominant role played by Vietnam in the area, one can

---

[1]"The Vietnam Agreement and Protocols", The New York Times, January 25, 1973, p. C15.

[2]"Text of Accord Between Lao Government and Pathet Lao", The Washington Post, February 23, 1973, p. 17.

postulate that once Saigon and Hanoi engage themselves in a meaningful scheme of economic interchange, autonomous forces will be generated from that cooperation leading toward restoration of the former Indochinese Economic Union within a relatively short period of time.

It is obvious that the Union, once established, will benefit each of its members economically. To the extent that economic cooperation may create a favorable environment for regional stability, the Union is likely to benefit its members politically as well.

From the outset, however, it seems important to point out that the whole question of normal relations between the two Vietnams and thus the future of Indochinese cooperation appears to rest on one crucial factor: the willingness of North Vietnam's leaders to respect the sovereignty and independence of South Vietnam and the other Indochinese states. That condition requires that North Vietnam withdraw its armed forces from South Vietnam, Cambodia, and Laos and agree to coexist peacefully with its neighbors.

In terms of the Paris Agreement, North Vietnam's willingness to adhere to Article 15(b) is of paramount importance. Article 15(b) declares that "North and South Vietnam shall respect the Demilitarized Zone on either side of the Provisional Military Demarcation Line."[3]

It seems clear that once provision (b) of Article 15 is honored, provision (c) of the same Article (on re-establishing normal relations within Vietnam) can certainly be materialized. It can be argued that economic relations among the states of Indochina, particularly between the two Vietnams, are not only desirable but also inevitable. That this is a valid contention can be supported by historical evidence.[4]

A tragedy which took place in North Vietnam in 1945 is sufficient to

---

[3]The New York Times, *op. cit.*

[4]The following section is based mainly on Chapters 2 and 3 of the author's book on The Economic Development of North Vietnam, to be published by Praeger.

For convenience of reference, the following terminologies are used in this paper: North Vietnam (NVN) or Democratic Republic of Vietnam (DRVN) or the North. Unless otherwise qualified, this refers to the area above the partition line at the 17th parallel. It includes Bac Bo (Tonkin) and four northern provinces of Trung Bo (Annam). South Vietnam (SVN) or Republic of Vietnam (RVN) or the South refers to territory below the 17th parallel. It includes Nam Bo (Cochinchina) and the southern provinces of Trung Bo (Annam).

illustrate the impact of the breaking-up of Vietnam's economic unity. During that year when the traditional rice supply from the Mekong Delta to North Vietnam was discontinued because of damage to the transportation system and disruption of French administrative control, there was mass starvation in the Tonkin Delta resulting in the loss of between one and a half and two million lives (or about seventeen percent of North Vietnam's population at the time). The crisis was so serious it affected the very center of Hanoi.[5]

Because of demographic pressure and the frequent flooding of the Red River, North Vietnam has traditionally depended on Cochinchina (South Vietnam proper) to make up for its annual food deficit. The supply of food from South to North was the most important component in the traditional economic relation between the two Vietnams.

Economically, Vietnam is divided into two complementary regions, the industrialized North and the agricultural South. In pre-partition years, the South supplied the North with rice, rubber, and other agricultural products, while the North offered coal, cement, textiles, and other manufactured and chemical products in exchange. The North also sent large numbers of workers to the South to earn their living while providing some relief from population pressure. The French administration constructed an elaborate transport network to facilitate the intra-Vietnam flow of goods; the network included the coastal waters between Haiphong and Saigon ports, the Trans-Vietnam (*Xuyen-Viet*) railroad (2,800 kilometers in all Indochina, of which the Hanoi-Saigon line totaled 1,900 kilometers), and Route One (2,600 kilometers in all Indochina, of which about 2,000 kilometers were in Vietnam).

On a national scale, the distribution of agricultural resources weighs heavily in favor of the South while the end output of industrial materials is the monopoly of the North. Table 1 illustrates the difference in the

---

[5]The discontinuation of paddy supply from the South to the North was due to the breakdown of the transport and marketing system. In addition, paddy availability in the South also declined during World War II when the Japanese and Vichy French administrations confixcated a large quantity for their own reserves. *See* Girard Chaliand, The Peasants of North Vietnam (Middlesex, England: Penguin Books. Ltd., 1969), pp. 34-34; for a detailed description of the crisis *see* Françoise Martin, Heures Tragiques au Tonkin (Paris: Berget-Levroult, 1948), pp. 99-105.

Table 1

DISTRIBUTION OF POPULATION, CULTIVATED LAND, AND PRODUCTION OF
MAJOR COMMODITIES IN NORTH AND SOUTH VIETNAM IN SELECTED YEARS

| | NORTH | | SOUTH | | TOTAL VIETNAM |
	Quantity	Percent of Total	Quantity	Percent of Total	
1942:					
Population (thousands of people)	12,550[1]	59	8,900[2]	41	21,450
Cultivated Area (thousand hectares)	1,925	41	2,811	59	4,736
Paddy (thousand metric tons)	2,335	39	3,711[3]	61	6,046
Rubber (tons)	870	0	51,760	100	52,630
Coal (thousand metric tons)	2,329	100	0	0	2,329
Cement (thousand metric tons)	270	100	0	0	270
1955:					
Population (thousands of people)	13,574	53	11,948	47	25,522
Cultivated Area (thousand hectares)	1,600	42	2,179	58	3,779
Paddy (thousand metric tons)	2,080[4]	43	2,767	57	4,847
Rubber (tons)	0	0	66,336	100	66,336
Coal (thousand metric tons)	642	100	0	0	642
Cement (thousand metric tons)	9	100	0	0	9

[1] Of which Tonkin accounted for 9,920,000.

[2] Of which Cochinchina accounted for 5,400,000.

[3] Of which Cochinchina alone accounted for 3,179,000.

[4] Estimated.

Sources:
    Union Francaise, Haut Commissariat de France pour l'Indochine, Annuaire Statistique de l'Indochine, Vol. X (1941-42), pp. 87-88; Vol. XI (1943-46), pp. 271-95.
    Democratic Republic of Vietnam, Central Statistical Office, So Lieu Thong Te (Statistical Data), Hanoi, 1953.
    U.S. Agency for International Development, Annual Statistical Bulletin, Saigon, 1960, pp. 4, 67-79, 97-101; also 1965-68, pp. 3, 85-99, 103, 130-39.

economic structures of the two regions prior to partition. In 1942, the last year for which complete data are available, the South with 41 percent of the total Vietnamese population held 59 percent of cultivated land, 61 percent of paddy, and 100 percent of the rubber production. The division left the North with only 39 percent of paddy to support 59 percent of the population. The Northern balance improved somewhat in 1955 after one million Northerners (roughly eight percent of the population) departed for the South under the free movement provision of the 1954 Geneva agreement.

Rough projections for 1975 show the North with 26,665,000 people, or 57.6 percent of the total for Vietnam, while its cultivated land only increases slightly to an estimated 2,500,000 hectares; the projected 1975 agricultural situation thus implies that each hectare of cultivated land in the North will have to support nearly eleven persons as compared with seven persons in the South (Table 4).

The most serious problem confronting Northern agriculture is that of sharp fluctuations in output from one year to another due to frequent calamities and the violence of the Red River's flow. Northern weather is well known for its extremes -- too much rain or too little, causing either flood or drought. The summer rains are often accompanied by great winds which turn into typhoons capable of washing away several dikes at one time and unleashing the river to destroy the entire crop.[6]

While the South can survive a poor harvest, a serious flood can bring about mass starvation in the North. In the physical environment of the Red River Delta, therefore, it is indeed the surplus of Southern rice shipped to the North which has traditionally brought relief to the Northern people.

Taking into account the complementary nature of the two economies, the free movement of commerce and labor, and the relatively sophisticated transport network, commercial relations between the two zones prior to partition appear to have accounted for an important part of the goods produced and consumed within each of the regions.

---

[6]For details on this point, *see* Pierre Gourou, The Peasants of the Mekong Delta, A Study of Human Geography (New Haven: Human Relations Area Files, Inc., 1955), Vol. I, pp. 61-64; also, Tran Dan Khoa, "Les Problèmes Hydrauliques au Nord Viet-Nam", in Etudes Vietnamiennes, Edition en Langues Etrangères, No. 2 (Hanoi, 1964), pp. 46-68.

Table 2

TRADE FLOW FROM NORTH TO SOUTH IN RELATION TO PRODUCTION AND
TOTAL EXPORTS IN SELECTED PRE-PARTITION YEARS[1]

	1939	1950	1951	1952	1953	1954
COAL (thousands of tons)						
Total Production	2,615	503	639	895	887	944
Percentage Exported	68	36	53	40	44	60
Total Exports	1,981	181	342	357	387	571
To South Vietnam	190	122	126	144	81	110
Percentage	10	67	37	40	21	19
Elsewhere	1,791	59	216	213	306	461
Percentage	90	33	63	60	79	81
CEMENT (thousands of tons)						
Total Production	306	144	212	225	291	225
Percentage Exported	81	66	51	44	49	51
Total Exports	247	95	109	100	143	130
To South Vietnam	90	78	97	95	142	130
Percentage	36	82	89	95	99	100
Elsewhere	157	17	12	5	1	0
Percentage	64	18	11	5	1	0

	1941	1942	1943
WORKERS			
Total Workers in Northern Mines	49,600	44,300	35,000
Net Outflow[2]	13,980	17,610	21,738
To South Vietnam	4,160	6,574	6,920
Percentage	30	37	32
Elsewhere	9,820	11,036	14,818
Percentage	70	63	68
Outflow as Percentage of Remaining Labor Force	28	40	62

[1]North and South Vietnam as defined by the 1954 Geneva Agreement.

[2]Net outflow of workers equals number of workers recruited from North Vietnam minus number of workers repatriated to North Vietnam.

Sources:
      Republic of Vietnam, Service de la Statistique Generale, Annuaire Statistique du Viet-Nam, Vol. I (1949-50), pp. 48-50, 116, 117, 128, 134, 135, 139, 257; Vol. II (1950-51), pp. 116, 132.
      Annuaire Statistique, op. cit. (p. 30), Vol. X (1941-42), pp. 283, 33, 188, 272, 278-79; Vol. XI (1943-46), p. 277; Vol. XII (1947-48), p. 113.
      Institute d'Emission des Etats du Cambodge, du Laos et du Viet-Nam, Compte Rendu des Operations (1954), pp. 91, 96.

Table 3

TRADE FLOW FROM SOUTH TO NORTH IN RELATION TO PRODUCTION AND
TOTAL EXPORTS IN SELECTED PRE-PARTITION YEARS[1]

	1939	1942	1950	1951	1952	1953	1954
RICE (thousands of tons)[2]							
Total Production	2,900[3]	2,543	1,036	1,249	999	1,003	1,043
Percent Exported	66	48	21	29	33	37	50
Exports	1,903	1,224	221	356	326	368	520
To North Vietnam	250[3]	250[3]	110	81	96	171	167
Percentage	12	20	50	23	29	46	32
Elsewhere	1,673	974	111	275	230	197	353
Percentage	88	80	50	77	71	54	68

	1939	1946	1947	1948	1949	1950	1951
RUBBER (tons)[4]							
Total Production	67,500	12,921	26,196	27,633	27,386	32,968	37,280
Percent Exported	--	--	--	--	105[5]	110[5]	99
Exports	--	94,682	35,813	29,606	28,797	36,267	37,109
To North Vietnam	--	167	135	581	139	128	142
Percentage	--	0.2	0.4	2	0.5	0.4	0.4
Elsewhere	47,541	94,515	35,678	29,025	28,658	36,139	36,967
Percentage	--	--	--	--	99.5	99.6	99.6

[1]North and South Vietnam as defined by the 1954 Geneva Agreement.

[2]Figures for Cochinchina only. Production and export figures are in tons of
rice. The conversion rate from paddy to rice is 0.65. Export figures for
1939-42 include some from Cambodia (about 8 percent).

[3]Estimated. For 1939 rice production, 2.3 million hectares x estimated
yield of 1.26 tons per hectare. United Nations, Toward the Economic Development of the Republic of Vietnam (New York, 1959), p. 33.

[4]Official data on exports were available for total Indochina, thus include
rubber shipments from Cambodia and Laos. In pre-partition times, however,
South Vietnam's production accounted for about 69 percent of total output
of Indochina. Therefore the "Exports Elsewhere" figures are calculated as
69 percent of total Indochinese exports.

[5]Exports were higher than production because they include stocking from
previous years.

Sources:
    See Table 2.

Table 2 illustrates the main features of economic interchanges between the two Vietnams prior to partition. The figures in this table can provide an approximation of the trade flow because of the fact that they are derived from different sources and are calculated from data originally given for the three zones of Vietnam and converted to fit the present-day division between North and South. Furthermore, they represent only the volume of controlled trade; that is, merchandise transported mainly by sea and railway between the points of loading and unloading. As such, the figures exclude "border" trade and some goods transported by road.

The North is well known for the richness of its sub-soil. Table 1 shows that in pre-war times, North Vietnam produced all of Vietnam's coal. Largely anthracite of high quality (relatively smokeless with low ash content), this coal is North Vietnam's most important mineral resource. Other less important minerals are iron ore, lead, phosphate, and gold. Some ninety percent of Indochinese mines are located in Tonkin (the rest in Laos). The mines, situated near sea ports and railways, provide employment for the majority of workers in the modern sector.

Coal represents the bulk of North-to-South trade. The deposits at Hon Gay and Dong Trieu were the largest mines in Southeast Asia. Prior to the French conquest of Indochina, the Chinese had long exploited coal mining in North Vietnam, though on a very small scale. It has also been argued that the richness of the Northern mines was among the main factors responsible for French interest in conquering Indochina.

During the colonial era, coal was extracted mainly for export to areas outside Indochina; nevertheless, "exports" to the South did occur. In 1939, total exports amounted to 76 percent of production, of which an estimated 190,000 tons (ten percent) were shipped to the South.

The volume of Northern coal consumed in the South appears to be very important when Northern shipments are compared with total imports of coal from foreign countries. In 1939, for example, total coal imported by Cochinchina from other sources (mainly Japan and India) amounted to only seventeen percent of the amount imported from North Vietnam. In 1950 and 1951 Northern coal shipments to the South were more than ten times South Vietnam's coal imports from the outside world.

Since 1954, the South has been cut off from its traditional fuel supply and has had to increase its imports from abroad -- as much as 67,880 tons in 1958.[7]

The availability of coal as a source of fuel permitted North Vietnam to undertake other industrial enterprises; among them, the cement industry was the most important. The cement plant at Haiphong, one of the largest factories in all of Indochina, was founded as early as 1899. It benefited from an abundant supply of raw materials (coal, limestone) situated nearby and from its location near sea and river transport facilities. While North Vietnam's coal production was mainly exported abroad, cement production played a larger role in Indochinese consumption. Of the total exported in 1939, 36 percent went to the South, mainly for use in the construction industry. During 1950-51 almost the entire amount of Northern cement exported went to the South. The volume of South Vietnam's cement imported from foreign countries in those two years represented only nine percent and 42 percent, respectively, of Northern shipments.

Other products reaching Southern markets from the North included minerals such as tin, zinc, iron ore, phosphate, and apatite (a crystalline phosphate of lime). In 1942, Tonkin produced 99,000 tons of apatite, 16,000 tons of zinc, 500 tons of tin, 13,000 tons of bauxite and -- together with Annam -- 62,000 tons of phosphate, 63,000 tons of pig-iron, and 1,438 tons of manganese. Half of these materials produced were exported, a significant amount no doubt reaching the Southern market.

In addition to the trade flow, movement of Northern workers to the South had a special role in the economic relationship between

---

[7]U.S. Operations Mission in Vietnam, Annual Statistical Bulletin (Saigon, 1960), p. 106.

the two regions.

The history of Vietnam has one similarity to that of the United States; it is a history of continuous migrations -- southward in the case of Vietnam. Whereas gold and land were the moving forces in the United States, in Vietnam it was the food supply of the Southern delta. To a Northerner, the image of the South has always been one of hope, of life; the river there is calmer, the land more bountiful. The Northern peasant even considers the wind which comes from the South more pleasant than the cold wind in the North. An architectural principle in the North is, "To build your house facing the South is as natural as to marry a woman" (*Lay vo dan ba, lam nha huong Nam*).

In 1943 the net outflow of workers from North to South was 21,738, compared with 13,980 in 1941 and 17,610 in 1942. This represented an average increase of nearly 25 percent per year. Averaging for 1941-43, the number of workers departing from North Vietnam corresponded to nearly 42 percent of the remaining workers who were engaged in mining, the most important activity in the modern sector.

As illustrated in Table 1, approximately sixty percent of the rice growing area and the rice production of all Vietnam is concentrated in what was Cochinchina, the southern part of the country. In the thirties, Cochinchina alone exported around 1.5 million tons of rice annually, about one-fourth of the world's rice exportation. In addition to export to foreign countries, Cochinchina sent about 250,000 tons of paddy to the rest of the country.

Data are not available to estimate with any precision the annual flow of Southern rice just prior to partition. Fragmentary information from both Communist and free world sources indicates that between 200,000 and 250,000 tons of paddy per year were sent to Tonkin alone. Table 2 provides partial data for paddy trade in selected years.

From an estimated high of 250,000 tons in the thirties, Southern shipments fell to 81,000 tons in 1951, then increased again to 171,000 and 167,000 tons in 1953 and 1954. The sharp decline was due to the reduction of production in the South because of deteriorating security conditions in the early fifties; the decline was also due to the breakdown of the North-South railway network during World War II. Southern shipments to other areas of Vietnam were very significant, especially in the early 1950's when Northern production was seriously reduced because of war. Thus in 1950 and 1953 rice shipments to the non-Communist areas in North Vietnam amounted to fifty and 46 percent of total Southern rice exports, compared with only twelve percent in 1939.

When the shipments are calculated on a quarterly basis, it appears that the largest rice shipments normally take place in the critical period before the Northern harvest. in 1953, for example, 32 percent of the year's shipments arrived during the rice transplanting period of the summer crop (mid-January to early March); in the following year, 41 percent arrived during the transplanting phase of the winter crop (end of June to early August). This was because food reserves in North Vietnam usually reach low points around February-April and July-September.

In relation to North Vietnam's rice production, the food "imported" from the South was very important although it varied from year to year depending upon agricultural performance in the North.

Other foodstuffs included in the South-to-North trade were sugar, tobacco, peanuts, vegetable oils, and beverages.

To North Vietnam, partition meant that beginning in July 1954 it could no longer depend on the South for yearly relief. The food shortage situation at the time of division was further aggravated by the disruption of production and marketing during years of hostilities in the Tonkin Delta and by natural calamities during 1954 and 1955. Only with substantial grain assistance from the Communist countries was widespread famine averted. In 1955 alone, the Soviet Union sent 170,000 tons of rice and China 50,000, making a total of 220,000 tons. It is interesting to note that the latter figure corresponds roughly to the annual flow of paddy from the South in pre-war years.

In order to speed up production, the Communist regime launched

an all-out effort to mobilize the entire population and to institute
fundamental reforms in the agricultural sector. Land reform was
doomed, however, as peasants reacted with anger to the application
of harsh measures of enforcement. As a consequence, in spite of
the expansion of cultivated area, agricultural production failed
to increase significantly enough to support a population that was
growing at a rate of 3.5 percent per year.

It is not possible to estimate precisely the output of paddy in
the North; the official data are at best ambiguous and generally
inflated. The government laid down ambitious targets for rice production in the 1958-60 plan and for the Five-Year Plan amounting to
7.6 million tons and seven million tons respectively. A target of
five tons per hectare was fixed for the "catch-up plan", 1966-67.
Actual production as officially claimed for each year ranged from
4.1 million tons in 1956 to 5.2 million tons in 1959, and five million tons in 1960. However, in view of the failure in agricultural
policies, the limited availability of land, and natural calamities,
the four- to five-million ton range appears to be exceptionally
high.

On the basis of my own estimates, the amount of paddy output
in North Vietnam during the sixties was in the neighborhood of between three and 3.5 million tons per year, a level which implies
an annual deficit of between one and two million tons, depending
on the outcome of each year's crops. The estimate of three to 3.5
million tons appears to correspond closely to the actual rice consumption in North Vietnam. In 1967, for example, the per capita
rice ration was about 13.5 kilograms per month, or 162 kilograms
per year. Taking into consideration the population of about twenty million in that year, total rice consumption was 3.2 million
tons. The three to 3.5 million ton output must, therefore, have
been the criterion of the planners in establishing the Northern
per capita rations. In order to make up for the paddy deficit, the
government resorted to external aid, imports, and to secondary crops.
Hanoi has vigorously pushed the cultivation and consumption of other

staple foods such as corn, sweet potatoes, beans, and manioc. However,
the move has been highly unpopular with the North Vietnamese people
who have often found more than half of their "rice" ration to be
composed of other, less welcome foodstuffs.

Professor P. J. Honey, noted author on North Vietnam, once
wrote about a joke that was going around in Hanoi during the summer
of 1961:

Q. The Party has at last found the only long-term solution
for our food problem. Do you know what it is?

A. Capture South Vietnam.

More than anyone else, North Vietnam's leaders realize the far-
reaching implications of the food crisis. Throughout the colonial
war, the main theme of the campaign to mobilize public support was
centered on the issue of food. Farmers were told that rice was the
aim, Communism the means to achieve it. It is natural that when
victory over the French came in 1954, the leaders were under great
pressure to fulfill their promises to provide an adequate food supply for the populace. As Bernard Fall pointed out, during the period
between the Viet-Minh revolution and the division of the country
(1945-54), the Communist Party could still blame any economic crisis
on the French expeditionary corps and the war and could turn a crisis into an effective weapon of propaganda. Beginning in 1955, however, the regime had to assume "the full obligations of orderly government in the economic field. On its eventual success or failure
in providing people under its control with an adequate living may
well depend in great part the survival of the whole regime."

Fully aware of the vulnerability of Northern agriculture and
of the consequences of food deficits, North Vietnam's leaders turned
to the South as soon as their administration was established in
Hanoi.

The Observer, on March 20, 1955, reported a story about Phan
Anh, then Hanoi's Minister of Foreign Trade. In an interview, Phan
Anh said:

> "Rice! First and foremost there must be enough rice.
> But this year's crops . . ." He shook his head and

made a small decisive motion with his chopsticks.
"This country must be unified. They need each
other economically, the North and the South.
There can be no question of continued partition."

As early as February 4, 1955, seven months after the partition
of the country, Hanoi proposed the restoration of "normal relations"
including postal exchange and sea, air, and railway transport between
the two zones.

Given the shaky state of security in the South during the years
following the division of the country and on account of bitter exper-
iences between Nationalists and Communists in the past, it was only
natural that the response from President Ngo Dinh Diem was negative.

Furthermore, there was a fear at the time that the trade proposal was only a scheme to permit Northern soldiers to infiltrate
the South for subversive purposes.

According to a North Vietnamese publication, Hanoi officially
proposed a conference to negotiate economic relations between the
two zones on June 6, 1955.[8] The negotiations were to begin on July
20. On July 19, one day before the proposed date of negotiations,
North Vietnam sent an official message urging the South to choose
"a meeting place on the territory of Vietnam to discuss the matter."
According to the same source, South Vietnam turned down the proposal
on August 9, 1955.[9]

An incident in Saigon in 1956 provides an important but neglected account of these economic negotiations. In that year, when
the food shortage in North Vietnam became critical, Hanoi sent a
special mission to Saigon headed by Van Tien Dung, one of the Dien
Bien Phu generals and later Chairman of the North Vietnamese Army's
Chiefs of Staff; he was to negotiate with President Diem for the
resumption of trade. Thousands of students staged anti-trade demonstrations and mounted an attack at the Majestic Hotel in Saigon

---

[8]Quang Loi, *Tam Nam Thi Hanh Hiep Dinh Geneve ve Vietnam* (Eight
Years of Implementation of the Geneva Agreement in Vietnam), (Hanoi:
Su That Publisher, 1962), p. 24.

[9]*Ibid.*

where the Northern delegation was staying.

Subsequent to the Dung mission, Hanoi re-approached the South on the same subject on March 7, 1958, and on October 4, 1960. According to Jean Lacouture, President Ho Chi Minh had expressed his desire on several occasions "to establish commercial relations permitting the North to buy rice from the South at a reasonable price."[10] In retrospect, it seems relevant to point out that it was only in December 1960, perhaps when the hope for trade with the South completely faded, that Hanoi launched the "National Liberation Front" as an instrument for total conquest.

By 1963, when the economic crisis was deepening due in part to serious drought and typhoons between the Spring of 1961 and Winter of 1962, Hanoi reportedly called again for trade between the two zones.[11]

In addition to economic trade, North Vietnam also wanted to negotiate monetary cooperation. In an article entitled, "The Struggle to Establish Monetary Relations between North-South", in Hanoi's Ngan Hang review, the complaint was made that the National Bank of South Vietnam had ignored four letters of the Director-General of the North Vietnam Central Bank proposing the establishment of monetary relations between the two zones; according to this document, the last letter was sent on November 11, 1958.[12]

The primary objective of the proposed monetary cooperation at that time was, however, to facilitate the transfer of funds by Southern Communists who had left the South and gone North after the 1954 cease-fire (i.e., those among the founders of the NLF) to their families still remaining in the South.

Whether these proposals were actually made is another question; the fact that the Director-General of North Vietnam's Central Bank took pains to report at length on the issue suggests that there was indeed pressure for such a course of action.

In light of the close economic link between North and South Vietnam in the past and considering the developments within the two zones since

---

[10] Jean Lacouture, "Uncle Ho Defies Uncle Sam", The New York Times Magazine, March 28, 1965.

[11] Far Eastern Economic Review, 1964 Year Book (Hong Kong, 1965), p. 236.

[12] DRVN, National Bank, Ngan Hang (Banking Bulletin), No. 12 (December 1958), p. 40.

partition, it seems realistic to suggest that, pending total reunification which will only be possible in the long run, the two Vietnams can coexist under arrangements for a partial unification following the German formula of "Two Zones in One Economic Entity".

That is to say, politically they may remain for the time being two separate states, but economically they can build a framework of joint economic cooperation eventually leading toward a common market for the well-being of all Vietnam.

That this is a real possibility can be supported by experience in Vietnam as well as elsewhere. In the past there had actually been a precedent involving economic trade between the Communist and non-Communist areas in Vietnam.

Prior to the 1954 partition, the country was already separated into areas controlled by Communists and by non-Communists. At the beginning of the Indochina war, the Communist Party maintained a policy of strict economic embargo *vis-à-vis* the non-Communist area. Later on, however, realizing the advantages of inter-zonal trade, this policy was completely reversed and trade between the two areas was actually advocated by the Viet-Minh.[13]

By virtue of a decree signed on August 13, 1951, the Communist Party laid down rather classic principles for trade with the non-Communist area, *viz.*, that the trade must (1) secure economic independence for the Viet-Minh zone, (2) protect its production, and (3) induce the import of what was strictly necessary while exporting only what was produced in surplus.

During 1951-52, the level of exchange between the two zones saw a five-fold increase; in 1953, exports from the Communist area to the non-Communist area increased further by 160 percent, while imports increased by forty percent.[14]

An important part of the trade took the form of bartering transactions; the rest involved the use of the currencies of the two zones -- the Indochinese Piaster and the Communist Dong. The exchange rates between the two

---

[13]Doan Trong Truyen and Pham Thanh Vinh, Building an Independent National Economy in Vietnam (Hanoi: Foreign Language Publishing House, 1964), p. 31.

[14]*Ibid.*, p. 32.

fluctuated widely from one region to another, and from one day to the next. As the Viet-Minh gained strength and their trade position improved, however, the Dong also increased in value. The exchange rate moved from one Piaster to between 48 and 100 Dong (depending on the region) in 1953 to about thirty Dong by the time of partition.

The two segments of population which were involved in warfare and territorial divisions and were also engaged in economic interchange at that time are also the two segments which now largely make up the people of North and South Vietnam.

In addition to the case of trade between the Communist and non-Communist Vietnams in the past, there is another case of economic interchange between two ideologically conflicting groups of people within the same country: the case of trade between the two Germanies.

The two Germanies remain politically separated, yet trade has flowed freely across the demarcation line since 1947. When the country was divided, East Germany was cut off from its traditional supply of coal, iron, and steel; West Germany, from sugar, wood products, and textiles. Trade between the two Germanies was established through a series of agreements signed in the late forties and early fifties.[15]

The amount and composition of trade is now determined each year between the *Ministerium für Aussenhandel und Innerdeutscher Handel* in East Germany and the *Bundeswirtschafts Ministerium* in West Germany. In East Germany, trade with the West is carried out by the State trade monopoly under the control of the Ministry for Foreign and Inter-German Trade which comprises twelve public trading firms. In West Germany, trade with East Germany is mainly in the hands of private traders, with quotas established for each commodity.

There is a real possibility that trade may finally emerge as one of the main components of peaceful coexistence in Indochina, because it enhances the spirit of cooperation. When trade finally does flow across the political barrier between the two Vietnams, the economic life of the entire Indochinese peninsula will be affected.

---

[15]For composition of East-to-West and West-to-East German trade in selected years, *see* U.N. Economic Commission for Europe, Economic Bulletin for Europe (Geneva), Vol. I, No. 2 (1949), pp. 26 and 50.

Trade is, of course, only a limited form of a broader scheme of economic cooperation. It is a polar case in a process toward a wide variety of commercial relations. For example, trade will require transportation which will necessitate repair of the Saigon-Hanoi railroad and Highway Route No. 1. Since the Hanoi-Saigon main roads and rails are also the main components of the trans-Indochina transport network, the transport facilities between these two capitals, once reconstructed, will eventually link other capitals -- Vientiane and Phnom Penh -- with Saigon and Hanoi as well.

Trade also requires the regulation of tariffs and payments, which in turn calls for restoration of the former customs and monetary union.

Looking at the prospects for cooperation in the years ahead, it seems clear that, once the two Vietnams re-establish normal economic relations, peaceful cooperation can be expected to contribute significantly to stability in Indochina and the rest of Southeast Asia as well. The immediate impact of such cooperation may set in motion powerful forces leading toward eventual reunion among the former French Indochinese states.

In recent years there has been a growing interest among Southeast Asian and world leaders in the feasibility of regional economic integration of the area's countries.[16] In the course of discussions about the subject, reference has often been made to a more desirable and realistic form of integration; that is, economic cooperation at the *sub-regional* level. While the Southeast Asian region is perhaps as a whole too large and heterogeneous to warrant early and far-reaching economic interdependent arrangements, it seems clear that obstacles to cooperation would be far less acute if the three or four countries of Indochina were to join each other in a mutually beneficial economic undertaking.

The United Nations' Consultative Group of experts on Regional Economic Cooperation in Asia put it this way:

> Apart, therefore, from the desirability of setting up a
> broad-based organization for regional cooperation, co-operative arrangements on a sub-regional basis will prove to be
> rewarding. These arrangements, which may be conceived on
> a horizontal basis, among groups of contiguous countries

---

[16]For a good summary of different schemes of integration in Asia, *see* Lalita P. Singh, The Politics of Economic Cooperation in Asia (Columbia, Missouri: University of Missouri Press, 1966), pp. 3-25.

can be depended on to provide for more effective integration of economic activities in well-defined fields of endeavour.[17]

It is reasonable to assert that, among the countries in Southeast Asia, the former French Indochinese states have the best chance of success in any regional arrangement. The simple reason is that such a closely knit economic and customs union already existed among them for several decades in the rather recent past.

The Indochinese Economic Union's sphere of influence extended to nearly 286,000 square miles, an area a little larger than the states of California and Nevada combined (Table 4). In 1970 that area was inhabited by over fifty million people, two and one-half times the population of California. About 85 percent of the people were engaged in agricultural activities, mainly in rice cultivation. Total surface area under cultivation amounted to a man/land ratio of 6.7 persons per hectare. The estimated Gross National Product of Indochina in 1970 was U.S.$7 billion, and its per capita income U.S.$137.

In what way will economic linkage between the two Vietnams lead to an integration of the former French Indochinese economies? Given the tradition of cooperation among the four states in the past and the fact that the Union was only dissolved in 1954, it can be assumed that, once the relationship between them is restored, the other sets of relationships among the four states will gradually be re-established.

An economic marriage -- though only by convenience -- between the two Vietnam will certainly enhance prospects for economic reconciliation in Indochina because that arrangement will remove some of the existing barriers to cooperation in the area.

Experience in Asian cooperation in recent years shows that obstacles to successful economic integration may be groups under three main headings: psychological, economic, and political.[18] Psychologically, the Asian countries involved may not have a tradition or institutions for inter-regional cooperation; the people, therefore, do not have the habit of coop-

---

[17]The entire recommendation may be found in the United Nations' "Report of the Consultative Group of Experts on Regional Economic Cooperation in Asia" (C/CN.11/615).

[18]Lalita P. Singh, *op. cit.* (p. 44).

Table 4

INDOCHINA: MAIN INDICATORS

AREA AND YEAR	Area (sq. mi.)	% of Total	Population (thousands)	% of Total	Productive Population[1] (thousands)	% of Total	Agricultural Population (thousands)	% of Total	Cultivated Area (thousand ha.)	% of Total	GNP (millions $US)	% of Total	Per capita GNP
1970													
Laos	91,499	32	2,962	6	1,659	6	2,340	6	960	13	350	5	$120
Cambodia	66,658	23	7,485	15	3,967	15	5,614	13	2,410	32	970	14	130
North Vietnam	61,437	22	22,452	45	11,675	44	20,207	47	1,700	23	2,180	31	97
South Vietnam	65,999	23	17,333	34	9,013	34	14,733	34	2,430	32	3,500	50	202
Total Indochina	285,593	100	50,232	100	26,314	100	42,899	100	7,500	100	7,000	100	$137
1975 (Projected)													
Laos	91,499	32	3,351	6	1,877	6	2,647	6	1,074[2]	5	432	5	$130
Cambodia	66,658	23	8,761	15	4,643	15	6,570	15	2,584	13	1,200	13	137
North Vietnam	61,437	22	22,665	39	13,866	46	23,998	45	2,500	48	3,174	35	119
South Vietnam	65,999	23	19,610	34	10,200	34	16,673	33	2,719	33	4,157	46	212
Total Indochina	285,593	100	58,387	100	30,585	100	49,888	100	8,877	100	8,963	100	$154

[1] Between the ages of 15 and 64.

[2] 1970's area plus 114,000 hectares to be irrigated by power.

Sources:
United Nations, ECAFE, Economic Survey of Asia and the Far East, 1969, pp. 228-35; 1970, pp. 235-36.
USAID, Saigon, Annual Statistical Bulletin, 1965, pp. 85-89 and 138.
IBRD, World Bank Atlas, 1972.
Asian Development Bank, South East Asia's Economies in the 1970's, pp. 131-231.

eration with each other. Economically, the separate areas may not possess
a high degree of complementarity and may have a low level of inter-regional
trade, thus lack a fundamental requirement for success in any economic interchange. Finally, in the political arena, Asian countries present "a pano-
rama of heterogeneity and, at places, instability."[19] They are even frequently involved in armed conflicts of serious dimensions.

In the case of the Indochinese sub-region, however, those obstacles
appear to be less acute.

The Indochinese war, the root of economic separation, was officially
ended by the January 1973 Paris agreement, although fighting still continues. The energies devoted to ideological conflict between North and South
thus could be channeled into peaceful economic competition and cooperation
in lieu of armed conflict. The two Vietnams have agreed, at least in principle, on the neutrality of the region. Article 15(d) of the Paris Agreement stipulates:

> North and South Vietnam shall not join any military alliance
> or military bloc and shall not allow foreign powers to main-
> tain military bases, troops, military advisers, and military
> personnel on their respective territories.[20]

Article 10(b) of the Cease-Fire Agreement for Laos emphasizes the same
principle.[21] Thus, at least a framework to reduce regional political tension has been agreed upon.

The second factor, the psychology of cooperation, is not a problem in
Indochina. The effect of cooperation between the two Vietnams will only
be to revitalize the traditional institutions of cooperation already established in the past. Although most Indochinese people condemn colonialism,
they still favor a certain degree of freedom of movement throughout the
former colonial area such as existed in the past.

Prior to the 1954 dissolution of the Indochinese Economic Union, the
four states -- North and South Vietnam, Cambodia, and Laos -- had achieved
a remarkable degree of integration. They had acquired a habit of cooperation; they had formed a customs union providing free movement of goods and

---

[19]*Ibid.*

[20]"The Vietnam Agreement and Protocols", *op. cit.* (p. 27).

[21]"Text of Accord Between Lao Government and Pathet Lao", *op. cit.*
(p. 27).

services among the territories; they had also adopted a common external tariff; a relatively sophisticated transport network including the Trans-Indochinese Railroad and Highway reinforced the tradition of interzonal trade. They also had a monetary union with a common monetary institute of issue and a common currency, and maintained a common central budget in addition to the territorial budget.[22]

Under the influence of the French administration, public administration, cultural institutions, and educational systems in all four countries resembled those of France, and French became the common official language. The background in cooperation still leaves visible imprints on the whole of Indochina. Thus, the problem of re-constituting the former union into a new one may not be as difficult as it seems at first glance.

Finally, as for the economic factor, the structure of Indochina's economies is such that possible gains through economic cooperation will be an important incentive to induce the Indochinese states to move toward a new economic union. This last point, the most crucial one in justifying economic cooperation, requires some elaboration.

One standard and critical requirement for the success of economic cooperation in any region is the existence of a certain degree of complementarity among the members' economies.[23] Compared with the economies of other groupings in Southeast Asia, such as those in the Association of South East Asian Nations (ASEAN) or the Regional Cooperation for Development (RCD), and others, the degree of complementarity of the Indochinese countries' economies is not smaller and has the potential of being much higher.

As shown in Table 5, North Vietnam has almost a monopoly in the area of mineral resources and has the potential of launching medium-sized industries such as iron and steel in addition to its present important output of coal and cement. In 1970, North Vietnam's production of coal and cement

---

[22]For more details about monetary and fiscal arrangements in the former French Indochinese Union, see A. Touzet, Federalisme Financier et Finances Indochinois (Paris: Recueil Sirey, 1935); Le Regime Monetaire Indochinois (Paris: Recueil Sirey, 1939).

[23]On the standard theory requirement of complementarity, see J. Meady, Problems of Economic Union (Chicago: University of Chicago Press, 1953).

Table 5

INDOCHINA: PRODUCTION OF SELECTED COMMODITIES*

AREA AND YEAR	Rice	%	Natural Rubber	%	Coal	%	Cement	%
1970								
Laos	932	8	--	--	--	--	--	--
Cambodia	2,253	20	43	60	--	--	50	5
North Vietnam	3,000	27	--	--	3,000	100	600	64
South Vietnam	5,115	45	28	40	--	--	286	31
Total Indochina	11,300	100	71	100	3,000	100	936	100
1975 (Projected)								
Laos	1,100	8	--	--	--	--	--	--
Cambodia	2,524	18	54	42	--	--	--	--
North Vietnam	4,600	32	--	--	4,000	98	750	79
South Vietnam	5,982	42	76	58	73	2	200	21
Total Indochina	14,206	100	130	100	4,073	100	950	100

*In thousands of tons.

Sources: See Table 4.

1975 projections based partially on past growth rates as follows:
   Population - growth rate for 1960-70.
   Productive Population - same percentage of population as for 1967.
   Cultivated Area - see note 2, Table 4.
   GNP - increased at same growth rate as average for 1960-70.
   Natural Rubber - for Cambodia, 1973 output projected to equal 1969
      level; for South Vietnam, 1963 level.
   Coal - for North Vietnam, 1973 output restored to 1965 peak level; for
      South Vietnam, restored to 1965 peak level during 1960's.
   Cement - restored to 1965 peak level.

was estimated at 3,000,000 tons and 600,000 tons respectively. Rough projections of its economic indicators indicate that by 1975 North Vietnam will at least be able to restore its 1965 peak level of 4,000,000 tons of coal and 750,000 tons of cement. Raw materials such as coal, tin, zinc, apatite, and iron ore and other industrial products such as cement, glass, and cotton are needed as inputs for the new manufacturing base in South Vietnam and to a smaller extent in Cambodia. In South Vietnam the industrial sector, which has grown fairly quickly during the war years, is now dependent entirely on foreign imports of raw and semi-processed materials, with the exception only of the cement industry. In addition to the food, beverage, and textile manufacturing sector, South Vietnam's industry now includes, among others, paper mills, chemical and plastic products plants, flour mills, and steel rolling mills. The relatively small but growing manufacturing sector in Cambodia, which includes glassworks, breweries, oil refineries, and steel wire factories, is also in need of North Vietnam's industrial inputs. In a few years Laos may also join North Vietnam in supplying tin and perhaps coal and iron ore to the region.

On the other hand, the ability of South Vietnam and Cambodia to supply North Vietnam's fast-growing population with food is obvious. In 1970, for example, the year when North Vietnam was not under intensive air war (*i.e.*, a normal productive year) and the fighting was continuing in South Vietnam and Cambodia (*i.e.*, a less-than-normally productive year), the estimated rice production in the North was only three million tons compared to 7.4 million tons in Cambodia and South Vietnam combined (Table 3).

As North Vietnam's population is growing at the fastest rate among the four Indochinese countries, projections for 1975 show an even wider gap in per capita food production between North Vietnam and the rest of Indochina. In two years, the Northern population will amount to 46 percent of the total for Indochina, while its rice production will only be 32 percent.

It seems relevant to point out that by 1975 when both North and South Vietnam will probably have brought all the land abandoned during war time into cultivation, the food production in Indochina as a whole will be just adequate to support its population; that is, the food surplus of South Vietnam, Cambodia, and Laos will be just sufficient to make up for North Vietnam's deficit (Table 6).

From a theoretical viewpoint, the case for economic cooperation may be

Table 6

INDOCHINA: THE FOOD BALANCE[1]

AREA AND YEAR	Population	Paddy Required[2]	Production	Surplus or Deficit
1970				
Laos	2,962	711	932	221
Cambodia	7,485	1,796	2,253	457
North Vietnam	22,452	5,388	3,000	-2,388
South Vietnam[3]	17,333	4,160	5,115	955
Total Indochina	50,232	12,055	11,300	-755
1975 (Projected)				
Laos	3,351	804	1,100	296
Cambodia	8,761	2,102	2,524	422
North Vietnam	26,665	6,400	4,600	-1,800
South Vietnam	19,610	4,706	5,982	1,276
Total Indochina	58,387	14,012	14,206	194

[1]Population in thousand persons; paddy in thousand metric tons.

[2]Paddy requirement for an average Vietnamese is estimated at 240 kilograms (equivalent to about 150 kilograms of rice) per annum.

[3]In 1970 South Vietnam still had to import rice despite surpluses in domestic production, due partially to bottlenecks in marketing and distribution during war time.

Sources: See Table 4.

built around the familiar theory of economic integration.[24] The theory emphasizes welfare gains and losses arising from the removal of trade barriers. When trade liberalization results more in "trade creation" (*i.e.*, when one member, *e.g.* Laos, can be induced to switch from high-cost domestic production in a field such as textiles to importation from a low-cost production such as North Vietnam's Nam Dinh textile mill) such economic cooperation will benefit both Laos and North Vietnam.

Much discussion on economic integration in recent years has centered around the dynamic effect of economic development and emphasizes the positive effects of the creation of a regional market.[25] The crucial advantage in this process is the widening of the members' markets, thus allowing their industries to enjoy the benefit of larger-scale production. Nearly two centuries ago, Adam Smith contended that the size of the market is the chief ultimate check on the development of high productivity. A quick glance at the economies of the four Indochinese states indicates that one of the main factors limiting investment in, and therefore development of, their industries has been the small size of the markets.

In 1970, for example, the population of Laos was less than three million; Cambodia, 7.5 million; and South Vietnam, 17.3 million. But together, the population of the whole Indochinese market was 50.2 million, roughly equal to that of France. By 1975 that population will reach 58.4 million. At the present stage, a major part of the manufacturing sector in Laos and Cambodia may be characterized as "cottage" industry, carried out wholly or partly within the family; another small portion is characterized as "small-scale" industry, using about fifty workers or less per establishment. Only in a very few instances does the number of workers per factory rise above the one hundred mark. The manufacturing sector in South Vietnam is also of the "cottage" type. In 1964, for example, a total of 11,840 manufac-

---

[24]For a good summary of the theory of integration, *see* R. G. Lipsey, "The Theory of Customs Union: A General Survey", The Economic Journal, Vol. LXX (September 1960), pp. 496-513.

[25]The effects of widening the market resulting from economic integration would be to offer possibilities for economies of scale. Various examples in Asia, Africa, and Latin America are cited in the author's article "Economies of Scale and Economic Integration", Finance and Development (Washington, D. C.: International Monetary Fund and World Bank, June 1968), pp. 35-40.

turing companies in the Saigon-Cholon area employed 113,900 persons, an average of 9.6 workers per company.

In addition to the benefits of economy of scale, a widening of the regional market may enhance the opportunities for profitable foreign investment and consequently mobilize unemployed domestic resources and broaden the export base.

From the viewpoint of the aid-giving countries as well as international institutions, a regional or sub-regional "trade group" appears to be a better candidate for assistance than an individual country. This is evidenced by the tremendous growth in recent years of international financing of projects undertaken jointly by several countries. The Mekong project, the Asian Highway, and the Niger and Senegal Rivers projects are only a few examples.[26]

This last observation seems particularly relevant to the Indochinese states in the context of post-war reconstruction and development. The program of reconstruction which is just about to be launched presents the aid-giving nations and international institutions with a rare opportunity to stimulate a joint development endeavor. By setting aside a significant part their aid to finance selected joint projects, the spirit of cooperation will be enhanced among the Indochinese partners.

Perhaps it would be premature to consider the establishment of an Indochinese Economic Union for this year or next. What can be done immediately, however, is to create a framework conducive to the reactivation of the economic ties of the past. For example, selected regional projects may be singled out for multilateral financing, such as the Mekong projects, hydro-electric power sharing, and the trans-Indochina railroad. In the case of the Mekong project, although North Vietnam is not a riparian state, it will be extremely interested in electric energy generated by the Nam Ngum hydro-electric power dam in Laos because the distance between Nam Ngum and Hanoi-Haiphong is not great. All the major railroads and highways in Indochina, once connected with each other, could be repaired and maintained jointly

---

[26]For some details on the Mekong project, *see* C. Hart Schaaf and Russell H. Fifield, The Lower Mekong: Challenge to Cooperation in Southeast Asia (Princeton: Van Nostrand, 1963). About the Niger River and Senegal River projects, *see* United Nations Economic Commission for Africa, Reports of the First UN Africa Regional Inter-Agency Meeting (C/CN.14/404).

by one transport authority instead of four.

In final analysis, it seems clear that whether the four Indochinese states can come together to re-establish their past union will depend greatly on whether or not North and South Vietnam can cooperate with each other. As already pointed out, the resumption of economic cooperation between the two Vietnams depends on only one crucial factor: the willingness of North Vietnam to accept a temporary division of the country and to respect the concept of "Two Zones in One Economic Unit".

But will North Vietnam be willing to settle for less than total unification? The answer to this question requires a thorough political and military analysis which obviously lies much beyond the scope of this paper, and ultimately the answer rests in the hearts and minds of the present Hanoi Politburo as well as in their successors.[27]

---

[27] As far as South Vietnam is concerned, an interest in resumption of commercial relations with North Vietnam has been expressed. In his October 31, 1971, inaugural speech, President Nguyen Van Thieu declared: "Pending unification, in order to maintain peace and to create favorable conditions for the reunification of the land, the two zones -- North and South -- despite their differences in regime, in policy, in ideology, can begin by exchanging letters, visits, to be followed by trade and economic exchanges in the spirit of 'two zones in one economic entity,' and compete in the building and in the task of bringing happiness to the Vietnamese people." Embassy of Vietnam, Press Release, November 1, 1971, p. 4.

V: THE VIETNAMESE IN CAMBODIA, AND THAILAND:
Their Role in Interstate Relations*

Peter A. Poole

During the 1950's and sixties, major powers seeking to influence events on the Southeast Asian mainland compiled bulky dossiers on the role of ethnic minority groups. Before long, the way in which certain countries viewed the minorities became a more important political reality than the minorities themselves.

Of particular interest were the overseas Chinese and Vietnamese, the *avant garde* of two Asian cultures apparently seeking to dominate Indochina. However, of the two groups, the Vietnamese (in Cambodia and Thailand) received the least attention.[1] When foreign reporters and local officials described them it was usually as a "fifth column" poised for a signal from Hanoi to begin destroying the societies they had infiltrated. They were not encouraged to assimilate (and were thought incapable of doing so); moreover, repeated efforts were made to expel them *en masse*.[2] Almost no

---

*This paper appeared as an article in Asian Survey, April 1974. It has been slightly revised. It is used here with the permission of the original publisher, California University Press.

[1] For a preliminary study, *see* Peter A. Poole, The Vietnamese in Thailand, A Historical Perspective (Ithaca, N. Y.: Cornell University Press, 1970).

[2] About 45,000 Vietnamese were repatriated to North Vietnam from Thailand between 1949 and 1964; there were an estimated 86,000 Vietnamese still in Thailand in 1973. See Tables 3 and 6 (pages 65 and 93) of The Vietnamese in Thailand (fn. 1) for the basis of these figures through 1967. A 2.5 percent annual net increase in the Vietnamese community is assumed for the years 1968-1973. This is lower than the 3% figure assume for 1946-67, because intermarriage created a drain of unknown but substantial size during the later period.

In public statements, Thai officials tend to estimate the number of Vietnamese refugees in Northeast Thailand at about 40,000 -- the number remaining when repatriation ended in 1964. However, the Far Eastern Economic Review (April 30, 1973, page 27) quoted a senior Thai official in Bangkok as estimating that there were "around 70,000".

About 200,000 Vietnamese were repatriated from Cambodia to South Vietnam during 1970. On the basis of the very limited data available, this writer estimates that there were 100,000 to 150,000 Vietnamese in Cambodia and 20,000 to 30,000 Vietnamese in Laos in 1973.

one bothered to consider the alternative possibility: that a more positive approach toward the Vietnamese minority groups might help to reduce the tensions in interstate relations.

A search for realistic attitudes and policies toward the Vietnamese minorities, particularly the large groups in Thailand and Cambodia, seems long overdue. Just as major power intervention tended to polarize the region along ideological lines in the fifties and sixties, so the military disengagement of the great powers now makes possible, indeed essential, a more objective and realistic approach to interstate relations. However, where traditional racial antagonism has long been reinforced by cold war rhetoric it is not surprising to find objectivity in short supply.

During the past fifteen or twenty years, the attitude of host governments toward the Vietnamese minorities has been consistently more negative than their attitude toward the overseas Chinese. This was not always true, however. The Vietnamese settlers were once more or less taken for granted; and there was a long history of friction between Chinese settlers and local elites from the revival of Chinese nationalism until about the time of the Bandung conference (1955). But beginning in the late 1950's, the governments of Thailand and Cambodia began to come to terms with the overseas Chinese. Among other things, they found that they had the means of countering Chinese Communist or Kuomintang subversion by manipulating the Chinese resident' legal and economic status. The realization that such pressures produce counterpressures seemed to limit the activity of all parties concerned.

From the 1930's to the early 1950's, "assimilation" often meant enforced conformity with local norms. But in the late fifties and sixties, it began to connote a more positive acceptance of the Chinese settlers into the mainstream of local societies. Occupational restrictions were reduced, and intermarriage became more common. There was a growing recognition that the overseas Chinese and the local societies had a good many interests in common.[3]

On the other hand, pressures on the Vietnamese minorities by the Thai

---

[3]*See* William G. Skinner, Chinese Society in Thailand: An Analytical History (Ithaca, N. Y.: Cornell University Press, 1958); and William E. Willmott, The Chinese in Cambodia (Vancouver: University of British Columbia Publications Centre, 1967).

and Cambodian governments have historically invited counterpressures by Hanoi and Saigon. While it is still not difficult to find Thai or Cambodian officials who are prejudiced against the overseas Chinese, few would go so far as to urge repatriating them to China. To begin with, there are simply too many Chinese to make such a plan worth considering.[4] However, both the Thai and Cambodian governments have at one time or another sought to repatriate all or many of their Vietnamese residents, in spite of serious practical obstacles. Experience has shown that the Thai or Cambodian governments cannot rid themselves of any substantial numbers of Vietnamese without the cooperation of North or South Vietnam. And they cannot hope for such cooperation without entering into arrangements with one of the two Vietnams that may be more distasteful than the minority group's presence. There are certainly some Thais who feel this way about their 1959 agreement with Hanoi, and there are some Cambodians who believe that their 1970 accord with Saigon led to undesirable entanglements.[5]

In addition, many of the Vietnamese in Thailand and Cambodia have no roots in any part of Vietnam and no desire to go there while the country remains in a state of upheaval. This is particularly true of the Vietnamese now living in Thailand, almost all of whom were born in Laos, Thailand, or Cambodia.[6] Besides, there is abundant evidence that the governments of Cambodia, Laos, and Thailand all lack the means to prevent illegal immigration of Vietnamese (or anyone else) into their countries. For at least a century and a half, beginning with the religious persecutions under Emperor Minh Mang, Vietnamese have moved into Cambodia, Laos, and Thailand

---

[4] In the mid-1960's, there were about 2,600,000 ethnic Chinese in Thailand, 435,000 in Cambodia and 45,000 in Laos; *see* Lea E. Williams, The Future of the Overseas Chinese in Southeast Asia (New York: McGraw-Hill, 1966). These figures were probably somewhat higher by 1974 because of natural increase.

[5] The Bangkok-Hanoi agreement is described in The Vietnamese in Thailand (fn. 1). The more recent Cambodian-South Vietnamese accord is discussed below.

[6] During the late 1960's, I encountered some Vietnamese born within the last twenty years in Thailand who expressed a romantic wish to go "home" to Vietnam to search for their true identity. On the other hand, many members of the same generation of descendants of Vietnamese refugees in Thailand were melting into Thai society through intermarriage with Thais.

whenever conditions in their homeland drove them to it.

The reluctance of the North and South Vietnamese governments to accept large-scale repatriation of refugees has already been implied. Hanoi lacks surplus food, and neither country wants the administrative burden of housing and finding jobs for thousands of repatriates, most of whom are used to living comfortably. Moreover, Hanoi and Saigon may each view the settlement of Vietnamese in Cambodia (and to some degree those in Laos and Thailand) as laying the groundwork for eventual Vietnamese control of those areas.

This, of course, is a prime reason why many people in these three countries would like to be rid of the Vietnamese minorities. They want to block Vietnam's westward movement or at least delay it as long as possible. But what about the risk of being overwhelmed by Vietnamese subversion if they adopt a rigid stand toward Vietnamese immigrants? How do the dangers of this attitude compare with the risks of a more flexible approach, such as the one which they seem to have adopted toward their much larger Chinese minorities?

These are among the most basic and perplexing questions which the people of Cambodia, Laos, and Thailand face in the 1970's, and there are no simple answers to them. The penalty for taking the wrong course may be tragedy at one level or another. Thus, the need to look at the various alternative approaches seems clear. We will examine with special care the role of the minorities in Cambodia and Thailand -- in the context of interstate relations -- since the beginning of the Sino-American détente and try to project current trends into the short-term future. Of the three host countries, Cambodia has the largest Vietnamese minority group and has followed the most rigid policy. Thailand, being farther from the two Vietnams, has been able to experiment with a policy of greater flexibility. The Lao government has rarely shown much concern about regulating the status of its Vietnamese minority (which is also much smaller than the other two).

Cambodia and the Two Vietnams

Lon Nol's plan of stimulating anti-Viet Cong demonstrations in eastern Cambodia in February 1970 may have had Prince Sihanouk's advance approval. But it is much less likely that Lon Nol (or Sihanouk) foresaw the growth of these demonstrations into uncontrolled anti-Viet Cong riots in Phnom Penh in early March. Sihanouk knew that a younger generation of Khmer elite

members on both the left and right (still lacking Lon Nol's support) were
hoping to push him aside and gain the limelight. Thus, he was staking his
own future when he flew to Moscow and Peking to make a frantic last plea
for Soviet and Chinese aid in curbing Hanoi. His gambit failed because
none of the major powers were in any position to dictate the Cambodian
policy of their Vietnamese allies.

When Lon Nol finally decided to overthrow Sihanouk, no one knew what
the reaction of the Khmer people or of the Vietnamese Communist forces
would be. Nor is there yet any solid evidence that Lon Nol was given firm
assurances of American support by the Nixon administration. However, he
was banking heavily on American support as he maneuvered his small army
against the Viet Cong troops in eastern Cambodia to keep them off balance
as long as possible. He also crushed the first Khmer resistance groups
that showed themselves in the eastern provinces. At the same time, the
coup leaders made an all-out bid for the support of the educated elite in
the capital.

It was obvious that students and other potentially dissident Khmer
groups were eager to attack the Vietnamese community.[7] By recklessly in-
citing the Khmers against their own neighbors, the coup leaders displayed
extreme political insecurity and incompetence. In the *village catholique*
area of Phnom Penh, the largest concentration of Vietnamese in the city,
thousands of Vietnamese were attacked by mobs, and their property was
stolen or destroyed. In the eastern provinces, anti-Vietnamese rioting
continued for several weeks; many Vietnamese who were able to do so fled
into South Vietnam.

---

[7]According to official Cambodian census figures for the 1962 census,
there were 217,774 Vietnamese (and 163,115 Chinese) in a total population
of 5,728,771. Of the Vietnamese, 151,147 were classed as urban dwellers,
and 66,627 as rural dwellers. (See table appended at the end of this
study.)

Western writers on Cambodia estimated the size of the Vietnamese minority in the early 1960's at between 300,000 and 450,000. Cambodia's 1950
census put the size of the group at 319,596 in a total population of
4,073,967. *See* The Vietnamese in Thailand (fn. 1), pp. 130-33. There was
no known reason for a decrease in the size of the Vietnamese community in
Cambodia between 1950 and 1970; rather, there was empirical evidence of a
substantial increase. However, some people may have preferred to report
their nationality as Cambodian or Chinese rather than Vietnamese in 1962;
census officials may also have understated the size of the Vietnamese community.

Reports of massacres of Vietnamese residents in several areas were published by members of the large foreign press corps in Cambodia at the time. (The reports were corroborated by interviews the present writer held in Phnom Penh eight months later with people who witnessed the events.) This publicity led to angry student demonstrations in Saigon, which the Thieu government found it difficult or impolitic to control. By early April 1970, public opinion in South Vietnam and the United States (the two countries to which Lon Nol looked for military support) had swung sharply against his regime. Many South Vietnamese officials favored moving the war westward at this stage, on the grounds that it was Cambodia's turn to bear the brunt of fighting.

With its position deteriorating rapidly, the Phnom Penh government sought massive military aid from Washington and help from Saigon in solving the Vietnamese problem. Saigon's leaders were the first to respond. They were quick to see the political and military advantages to be gained by turning Cambodia into a protectorate. Within a few weeks after the reported massacres, a high-level South Vietnamese official came to Phnom Penh to help arrange the repatriation of 200,000 Vietnamese who had taken refuge in make-shift camps.[8]

Saigon promptly agreed to help the Khmer government cope with its self-generated problem with the Vietnamese community in spite of having long resisted the idea of repatriating a much smaller group of Vietnamese in Thailand. The reasons for this were probably threefold: (1) the refugees in Cambodia were mainly of Southern origin; (2) it obviously was no longer safe for them to remain in Cambodia; and (3) South Vietnam derived some political and moral credit in the eyes of other peoples by accepting re-

---

[8]Shortly after Sihanouk's overthrow, Cambodia and South Vietnam resumed diplomatic relations, and the latter established an embassy in Phnom Penh with a large and active military liaison mission (which exercised wide responsibilities during 1970 and 1971), an information service, and a consular service. Relations between Phnom Penh and Saigon had been broken off in 1963, after Cambodia recognized the Democratic Republic of Vietnam and the Provisional Revolutionary Government of South Vietnam. This meant that the Vietnamese in Cambodia (who were mainly Southerners with a high percentage of Catholics) were exposed to direct and often unwelcome pressures by the Vietnamese Communists. Khmer elite members who had begun to question Sihanouk's conduct of foreign affairs thus had some grounds for being increasingly concerned about Communist subversion among the Vietnamese minority during the 1960's.

sponsibility for them.[9] None of these considerations applied in the case
of the Vietnamese in Thailand. There, the Vietnamese were not endangered;
and being mainly of Northern origin, they had no ties in the South and no
desire to go there.

Most of the Vietnamese in Cambodia were terrified by the massacres and
alleged massacres which took place during March and early April, and were
more than willing to leave Cambodia by the safest means available. Many
who were able to do so simply fled across the border into South Vietnam.
But a larger number sought temporary safety, while awaiting repatriation,
in make-shift camps or centers established by the Lon Nol government. Although no small measure of blame for the refugees' plight belonged to the
Phnom Penh regime, within this context it was true that these camps were
established for the safety of the refugees and that the repatriation was
essentially voluntary. The facilities provided for Vietnamese refugees
awaiting repatriation were no worse, and often better, than those provided
for Khmer refugees in the war-torn country. On arrival in South Vietnam,
the Vietnamese repatriates often faced another long wait in camps operated
by the Saigon government until housing and jobs could be found for them.[10]

During 1970 and 1971, all parties in the Vietnam struggle chose to
fight the war on Cambodia's territory. One major result of this was to
create a serious threat to the long-term security of Thailand (the main
non-Communist power center in the area) as the price of gaining a patched-
together peace in South Vietnam. This fact, added to the Sino-American

---

[9]U.S. officials also played an important behind-the-scenes role in
persuading the Cambodian and South Vietnamese governments to resolve the
issue as amicably as possible. However, the Nixon administration, apparently to avoid domestic political controversy, avoided making any long-term
commitment to the defense of the Lon Nol government.

[10]An agreement was reached between the Phnom Penh and Saigon regimes
making the former responsible for the refugees' unsold property in Cambodia.
But it is doubtful if many refugees benefited from this accord, most of
them having been forced to abandon their immovable belongings to looters
or sell them at a fraction of their value. At Saigon's insistence, a few
Vietnamese former residents were allowed to re-enter Cambodia in order to
tend to certain business interests there.
Vietnamese numbering 121 (including about 40 women and 50 children)
were released from prison in Phnom Penh and flown to Saigon on May 15, 1973.
A New York Times report on that date said most of them had been imprisoned
in Phnom Penh just after Sihanouk's overthrow on charges of collaborating
with the Vietnamese Communists.

détente, seemed to some Thai to call for a far-reaching re-evaluation of their country's defense policy.

Meanwhile, the Cambodians suffered even more directly when the war moved into their country. The rice and rubber economy was destroyed; between one and two million people were driven from their homes; and Cambodians lost all semblance of control over their own destiny as their country became a cockpit for proxy warfare between the two Vietnams, each backed by a major power. Indeed, it appears that the United States, the two Vietnams, and perhaps Peking and Moscow all believed, during 1972, that civil war in Cambodia was helping to bring about an acceptable conclusion to the struggle in South Vietnam.

The 1973 truce agreements on Vietnam and Laos and the bombing halt in Cambodia led to a reduction in outside (including DRV) support for the main Cambodian factions.[11] It seemed to be recognized by the major powers that none of them had anything to gain from a continuation of the war in Cambodia; if they wanted to persuade their Khmer clients to lay down their arms, the most obvious means would be to stop supplying them with ammunition.

Even if external arms shipments cease, however, the main impulse for political compromise and peace in Cambodia would have to come from the Khmer elite, which in late 1973 seemed as badly fragmented as ever. In this connection, it was interesting that Prince Sihanouk repeatedly disclaimed any wish to play the role of political leader of a reunified Cambodia; he said that he wanted to be Cambodia's chief diplomat and external spokesman.[12] Apparently the task of building a new political consensus would devolve on those younger members of the Khmer elite (on both sides in the current war) who had rejected Sihanouk's political leadership. A strong mandate from all the main factions of the younger generation elite would be needed by anyone, including Sihanouk, who might try to lead Cambodia out of its chaos.

Sihanouk's policy of leaning toward North Vietnam helped to keep

---

[11]One direct result of this was to bring into the open latent hostility between Prince Sihanouk and the DRV; there were also reports in 1973 of fighting between Vietnamese Communist and anti-Lon Nol Khmer forces in eastern Cambodia.

[12]See *Washington Post*, October 15, 1973.

Cambodia reasonably unified and isolated from the Vietnam war in the 1960's. However, few of the younger potential leaders on either side of the current struggle seemed likely to go to such lengths to conciliate Hanoi in the 1970's. At the same time, the Lon Nol regime had demonstrated that direct military confrontation with the Vietnamese Communists, coupled with a hard-line approach toward the Vietnamese minority in Cambodia, was a prescription for national suicide. Thus, the Cambodians would apparently have to find a way to deal with Vietnam and the Vietnamese minority which would fall somewhere between these two extremes.

Thai-North Vietnamese Relations

Both Hangkok and Hanoi were forced to adjust their foreign policies because of the relaxation of Sino-American tensions and U.S. military withdrawal from Indochina.[13] North Vietnam no longer had full Chinese backing for a high-risk policy. The Thai had never extracted an open and unconditional pledge of American military support. A substantial portion of the elite no longer seemed certain that this would be the soundest basis on which to rebuild their foreign policy; this fact was underlined by the overthrow of Marshal Thanom's government on October 14, 1973, after student rioting.

During the early 1960's, a war of nerves between Hanoi and Bangkok focused on the Vietnamese minority in Northeast Thailand. The DRV openly threatened Thailand with a subversive "war of liberation", apparently hoping to dissuade the Thai from granting air bases and other facilities to the United States. The Vietnamese minority, many of whom were employed in building and maintaining the air bases, appeared to be a made-to-order

---

[13]As U.S. forces withdrew from South Vietnam, the number of U.S. Air Force and other U.S. military personnel in Thailand remained at a level of 45,000 to 50,000. By 1972, this was the largest U.S. military concentration in Southeast Asia, and by mid-1973 the largest anywhere in the world except West Germany and perhaps South Korea. Negotiations to reduce the U.S. presence in Thailand began in the summer of 1973. Use of Thai bases for intensive bombing campaigns in 1972 and 1973 led former Foreign Minister Thanat Khoman to criticize his country's exposed position (for which he had been partly responsible). As Thanat's article in the June 7, 1973, New York Times pointed out, Thai leaders had never obtained any firm assurances of support from the United States. Yet they had allowed their basic foreign policy posture to become provocatively anti-Communist.

By 1974, it was evident that pressure for reducing the U.S. Air Force present in Thailand (and perhaps consolidating it at Sataheep-Utapao) was coming mainly from the Thai Foreign Ministry rather than from China.

instrument of sabotage and subversion. However, Thai leaders discovered that they could counter this threat by announcing every once in a while their willingness to deport the entire Vietnamese minority to a Thai island in the Indian Ocean. This would have been a blow to the prestige of Hanoi (the refugees' professed protector). Moreover, it would have eliminated a possible DRV auxiliary force in a strategic area.

Throughout the 1960's, Thailand and North Vietnam managed to avoid full-scale war, although their forces were in contact in Laos and South Vietnam, and most U.S. air attacks in Indochina were mounted from Thailand. Thai police occasionally jailed some of the refugees on charges of subversion; and pro-Communist refugees may have been responsible for a few attacks on Northeastern air bases. But neither side seemed willing to risk going further.

In the era of Sino-American détente, Thai leaders have used every available means to measure the real aims of other powers and to signal their adjustment to these aims. The Vietnamese refugees have sometimes served as an instrument for this purpose. For example, after the U.S. bombing halt in 1968, Deputy Premier Praphat signaled his concern by announcing the immediate resumption of talks with Hanoi on repatriation.[14]

As the pace of U.S. disengagement quickened, the same device was often used to remind Washington that the Thai expect to be consulted about decisions that affect their country's security. One of the worst instances of American negligence (in the eyes of Thai officials) occurred in February 1973, when Thai leaders received very little advance notice of the decision to move the Seventh Air Force and other major military commands from South Vietnam to Thailand. Shortly after learning this, Prime Minister Thanom told reporters that all of the Vietnamese refugees in Thailand would be sent to North Vietnam, implying that an agreement with Hanoi was more or less complete.

The Thai Deputy Foreign Minister underlined Bangkok's message to Washington. He told reporters on February 17, 1973, that the Thai government

---

[14] Praphat's message was presumably directed primarily at Washington, which may well have neglected to keep Bangkok fully informed of its thinking at this stage. It would be interesting to know what effect, if any, Praphat's statement had on the Thieu regime in December 1968.

was using three separate channels to contact Hanoi on the refugee issue:
ambassadorial talks in Vientiane, the International Red Cross Society, and
the good offices of UN Secretary-General Waldheim. He stressed that Thailand did not need or want to have Dr. Kissinger negotiate with Hanoi on
Bangkok's behalf because direct communication was proceeding between the
two Southeast Asian countries. He suggested that repatriation of the refugees, who were mainly well-educated and healthy individuals, would contribute to North Vietnam's reconstruction (the subject of the Kissinger-
Le Duc Tho talks being held at that moment). In short, the Deputy Foreign
Minister asserted that Thai and U.S. contacts with the DRV regime were on
parallel tracks.[15]

Shortly after the Vietnam truce agreement, the Thai government also
announced new efforts to promote trade with mainland China and the assign-
ment of commercial attachés to Saigon and Phnom Penh. However, Bangkok's
apparent aim of improving relations with the DRV and PRG (while continuing
to coordinate its policy with Washington) ran into difficulties during the
next six months. It was not clear whether the static was being generated
more in Bangkok or abroad. Hanoi seemed relatively unresponsive to Thai
overtures, probably because the DRV was much less politically isolated than
in the past. Peking seemed more receptive to Thai overtures than Hanoi.

However, some members of the Thai government indicated their fear that
moving too quickly toward détente with China would lead to increased Communist influence among the overseas Chinese in Thailand. (No doubt many
complex adjustments were taking place between overseas Chinese business
leaders in Thailand and various factions of the Thai elite as Bangkok gear-
ed itself for an expansion of trade with mainland China.) Under these conditions, it was hard to predict whether Thai officials might delay the establishment of full diplomatic and trade relations with China and North
Vietnam until they felt that the Chinese and Vietnamese minority problems
were under some kind of control.

However, it was obvious that delay on these issues was adding fuel to
domestic political criticism of the Thanom regime. Former Foreign Minister
Thanat's outspoken remarks have already been noted. During the spring and

---

[15]*See* Foreign Broadcast Information Service, Asia and Pacific Daily
Reports, February 20, 1973, pp. J2-J3.

summer of 1973, the military regime felt compelled to make many concessions to an increasingly organized and assertive Thai student movement, which seemed to have the tacit support of King Bhumipol and many civilian leaders. Marshal Thanom's position was not made easier by the fact that Thailand was also suffering from the worst inflation in many years, brought on by a series of calamitous droughts.

Above all, the prestige of the pro-U.S. military regime was badly undermined by mounting evidence (often supplied by its own spokesmen) that the Nixon administration was not consulting Bangkok before making decisions that deeply affected Thai security. General Kris Siwara declared in February that the American military presence in Thailand "gives us a warm feeling of security" but conceded that the numbers of American troops to remain in Thailand had not been fixed. (General Kris replaced Thanom as Commander-in-Chief of the Army a few months later; he failed to lead his troops against the Thai student demonstrators who overthrew Thanom in October and he seemed likely to play a prominent political role over the next few years.) In July 1973, the official Thai government spokesman complained to the New York Times that "Washington does not keep us informed" of its intentions (e.g., in regard to Cambodia). He pointed out that "before we can formulate our own policy we must know what the United States is planning."[16] It is difficult to know how clear it was to Thai military leaders, even at the time of the Cambodian bombing halt, that the Nixon administration was losing the initiative on Indochina policy to Congress. However, the subsequent overthrow of Thanom indicates that this fact was not lost on Thailand's civilian elite.

Meanwhile, the Vietnamese refugees were slowly being absorbed into Thai society, which offered greater material comfort and security than either of the two Vietnams. Bangkok, Hanoi, and Saigon were all virtually powerless to prevent this from happening. Saigon had the least leverage over the Vietnamese in Thailand and the least to gain from any country's manipulation of them. Thus, South Vietnamese diplomats had long urged the Thai to let law-abiding Vietnamese become permanent residents. At time of writing, the Thai government still offered no legal means for a refugee to

---

[16]New York Times, July 26, 1973.

become a permanent resident except by marrying a Thai citizen. Even if he were born on Thai soil, the child of Vietnamese refugee parents was classed as a refugee. However, there were signs that Thai officials might be experimenting with a pragmatic approach of not enforcing all the petty rules designed to remind a refugee of his status -- in order to see if they responded to positive inducements to assimilation.

Political developments in Laos during 1973 and 1974 suggested the possibility of an alignment of Chinese and American policies toward Southeast Asia (similar to their alignment in South Asia). Each would have an interest in preventing the DRV from dominating the whole Southeast Asian mainland (with Soviet support). If such a balance should emerge, one could foresee continued manipulation of the Vietnamese minority issue by Hanoi and Bangkok for long-established ends: to warn each other of the danger of precipitate action and to remind their allies not to take them too much for granted.

Appendix: VIETNAMESE IN CAMBODIA, 1950 TO 1973

REGION/PROVINCE	1950 Census (ethnic Viet.)	1962 Census (Viet. nationals)	1962 Est. (ethnic Viet.)	1973 Est. (ethnic Viet.)
Central Region				
Phnom Penh city	100,000	51,452	110,000	
Kandal (excludes Phnom Penh)	52,318	32,838	60,000	
Kompong Cham	31,564	25,872	40,000	
Kompong Speu	252	272	500	
Kompong Chhnang	16,773	15,007	17,000	
Total	200,907	125,445	227,500	100,000
Northeast Region				
Stung Treng (includes Ratanakiri)	2,636	1,137	3,000	
Kratie (includes Mondulkiri)	4,403	8,604	10,000	
Total	7,039	9,741	13,000	5,000
Southeast & South Region				
Preyveng	45,958	31,258	60,000	
Svayrieng	8,993	11,143	12,000	
Takeo	14,880	8,403	20,000	
Kampot (includes Kep, Bokor, & Kompong Som)	8,659	4,759	12,000	
Total	78,490	55,563	104,000	50,000
North & West Region				
Battambang	15,923	7,957	25,000	
Pursat (includes Tonle Sap Province & Koh Kong)	9,649	8,743	14,000	
Siem Reap (includes Oudar Mean Chey)	2,278	3,376	4,000	
Kompong Thom (includes Preah Vihear Province)	5,310	6,949	7,500	
Total	33,160	27,025	50,500	10,000
TOTAL, All Regions	319,596	217,774	394,000	165,000

Note on Sources:
   The 1950 census figures were prepared by the French colonial administration on the basis of estimates supplied by district officers (not on the
basis of a house-to-house canvass of all residents). Thus, the only biases
they would be likely to reflect would be those of French administrators

(not of the Vietnamese or the Cambodians); there is no obvious reason for the French administrators to understate or overstate the size of the Vietnamese community in Cambodia in 1950.

However, historical data and empirical observation strongly suggest that there was a substantial increase in the number of Vietnamese living in Cambodia between 1950 and 1962, both by natural increase and by an excess of entries over departures. Cambodia was safer than South Vietnam and offered attractive economic opportunities during much of this period; French economic establishments continued to prefer Vietnamese to Khmer employees.

For a number of reasons, therefore, it appears that the 1962 census figures greatly understated the actual number of *ethnic* Vietnamese in Cambodia at that time. Many ethnic Vietnamese adopted Cambodian nationality in order to be eligible for certain restricted occupations. However, they usually continued to think of themselves as Vietnamese; many of them did not make any effort to learn the Cambodian language, nor did they adopt the Cambodian form of Buddhism. Nevertheless, there were strong inducements for an ethnic Vietnamese (whether or not he had adopted Cambodian nationality) to describe himself as a Khmer to a census-taker. Popular prejudice against Vietnamese was reflected in serious street riots in Phnom Penh in 1962. Official prejudice was reflected in the reservation of certain occupations for Cambodians, in the frequent deportation of Vietnamese "trouble-makers", in official charges of Communist subversion among the Vietnamese, and in a steady stream of official propaganda against the Saigon regime. (Most of the Vietnamese in Cambodia were of Southern origin.) Since the Cambodian government, in 1962, was arguing its claim to portions of South Vietnam on the basis of the residence there of ethnic Khmers, it was not in Phnom Penh's interest to publicize the number of ethnic Vietnamese living in Cambodia.

The third column (1962 Est.) in the above table is an attempt by the author to adjust the 1962 census figures to show where the concentration of ethnic Vietnamese appears to be much higher than the census figures might indicate. These figures are based primarily on empirical observation by the author, who visited every province in Cambodia during 1961 and 1962. Figures in the right-hand column (1973 Est.), based on interviews in Cambodia in 1971-72 and press reports and interviews in Washington since then, attempt to reflect the large net outflow of Vietnamese from Cambodia between 1970 and 1973; these figures are admittedly only estimates.

VI: AMERICAN AND JAPANESE STRATEGIC PERSPECTIVES ON INDOCHINA

Bernard K. Gordon

The ceasefire agreements which were signed in Vietnam and Laos in
1973 brought to at least some sort of halt more than twenty-five years of
large-scale violence in those areas. They suggest that a watershed has
been reached in the international politics of East Asia. For the United
States and Japan, as for the other great powers with major interests in
East Asia, the seeming close of the Vietnam war may mean that new policy
departures are possible -- almost for the first time in the generation
since the end of the Pacific War.

There is little evidence in either Washington or Tokyo, however, of
an opportunity to be grasped or of new directions that should be laid out.
Instead, the strategic perspectives towards Indochina -- and Southeast
Asia generally -- of both countries seem characterized by uncertainty,
drift, and ambivalence. Even among those who recognize that the circumstances of East Asia may now justify or even require new American and
Japanese policies towards Indochina and Southeast Asia, no policy roads
seem especially well-lighted.

Even in the absence of clear policies, there are at a minimum some
basic considerations to which we can point. For American policy, at least,
it is clear that the United States did finally tire of twenty years of
heavy and direct military involvement in Southeast Asia. The action of
the Senate, and then of the House, in finally bringing to an end the American bombing effort in Cambodia, which became effective on 15 August 1973,
reflected the evident fact that almost all Americans regard as extremely
distasteful and highly improbable that the United States will again become
involved in Southeast Asian hostilities in the foreseeable future. Yet
even this has to be qualified, for American officials -- whether for bargaining purposes or as a matter of conviction -- seem much less positive
that the end of American military roles can be safely presumed.

Three illustrations can be mentioned. First, not only do White House
and other officials stress that the United States intends to hold on to
its air and naval bases in Thailand (although with fewer personnel than
before), but they have regularly left the door open for resumed use of

these bases should that become necessary for renewed operations in Vietnam and Laos. Then consider Cambodia. Direct support of the Cambodian govern-seems clearly inhibited by law, but several forms of indirect and "third party" arrangements have not been foreclosed. And finally, there are strong indications that the U. S. will make use of its Pacific "trust territories" for strategic purposes. Indeed, just as Thai-American agreements were announced for reducing American force levels from 45,000 to 32,000, and for other reductions in the American base structure in Thailand, other plans were announced in the Marianas to acquire two-thirds of Tinian Island -- for "construction of a major new military base."[1]

In Japan, leadership attitudes toward "post-Vietnam" Indochina show similar inconsistencies between involvement on the one hand and a continuation of "low posture" on the other. While for years Japanese leaders have been at pains to avoid political involvement in Southeast Asia (and particularly in Indochina), and have resisted all efforts to enlist their participation in the ultimate cease-fire arrangements, the Japanese became upset in 1972-73 that their disclaimers appeared to have been taken seriously. In November 1972, for example, Prime Minister Tanaka observed that "there cannot be any 'post-Vietnam' which excludes Japan."[2] This was followed a few weeks later by Foreign Minister Ohira who remarked that "nobody" thinks that an effective effort for rehabilitation can succeed in Indochina "without the participation of Japan."[3] Any speculation that these were isolated musings should have been dispelled soon afterward by a resentful speech that made major Japanese and American headlines: the Secretary-General of the governing Liberal-Democratic Party complained that "in the process of problem solving [on the future of Indochina], I

---

[1]Ambassador Haydn Williams announced to the people of the Marianas that the base would include an "airfield, harbor, training and maintenance facilities" (Reuters report in Christian Science Monitor, 23 June 1973). It needs to be recalled that Tinian, like Guam, is only about 1500 miles east of Manila. Similarly, the distance from the B-52 facilities in Thailand (at Sattahip) to Peking, for example, is near-identical with the distance from Tinian to Peking: about 2400 miles. For comparative purposes, this is precisely the flying distance between New York and Los Angeles; i.e., less than five hours even for the relatively slow B-52.

[2]Tanaka quoted in Nihon Keizai, 24 January 1973.

[3]New York Times, 26 January 1973.

do not remember any case in which we were properly consulted."[4]

These instances help to illustrate a more general proposition: that in both Washington and Tokyo there is wide vacillation on policies towards Indochina in the "post-Vietnam" era. Among Americans there is of course a desire to "get out" altogether, just as among some Japanese there are increasing signs of a willingness to "get in". But these prescriptions are contradicted by many in both capitals who argue that departures from the policies of the past two decades will bring greater problems than the traditionally maintained positions. While it is difficult to make a safe prediction of what posture ultimately will emerge from these contradictions, it is not too difficult to explain the present confusion among both Japanese and Americans.

The Americans, who want very much to reduce their political and certainly their military involvement in Southeast Asia, are worried that the appearance of a too-rapid disengagement will leave behind dangerous "vacuums". One quasi-humorous illustration of this point revolves now around the future of SEATO: while each of the remaining members in the Organization is evidently prepared to SEATO lapse, it is American spokesmen who have voiced the surprising desire that new life should somehow be breathed into the "alliance". Accordingly, State Department officials have regularly argued that "new purposes" should be found for the body -- presumably in the belief that this will help to convey the image of a continued American and "Western" presence in the region. The irony here is that SEATO's other members, for whose security the alliance presumably was established in the first place, recognize that the arrangement has outlived its usefulness and deters nothing. Accordingly, the Australians, Thais, and Filipinos who have suggested publicly that SEATO be allowed to die gracefully do not seem to fear that a "vacuum" will result if SEATO disappears; yet if the present United States view carries, this remnant of an earlier era will be around for the indefinite future.

A concern for "vacuums", but with a different twist, also contributes to Japan's lack of a clear-cut policy toward "post-Vietnam" Asia. But the

---

[4]Tomisaburo Hashimoto, quoted in the New York Times, 26 February 1973. The fact that the LDP Secretary-General spoke on this subject helps to indicate that the matter is of wide party concern, rather than only the particular point of the Tanaka or some other faction in the LDP.

fear that most exercises Tokyo is not that Japanese policies will create a
vacuum, but that Japan will somehow be "sucked in" to Southeast Asian defense problems if Tokyo admits to political interest in that region. Indeed, in recent years Japan's well-known economic dominance throughout
non-Communist Asia increasingly has impelled it to become further involved
in many Southeast Asian affairs, but the Japanese are extremely worried
that if they do become more active a trap door will close behind, not only
locking them in but leaving Japan with unilateral security expectations
that could lead to unacceptable defense obligations.

At the heart of the ambivalence among Japanese and American leaders
towards future Southeast Asian roles is the conviction -- at least among
their official establishments -- that the region (including Indochina)
does in fact bear importantly on their own security concerns. In Washington, this is partly a matter of a twenty-year experience that saw the U.S.
become deeply and intimately involved in the security concerns of at least
a half-dozen Southeast Asian nations, in an era when the security of those
small states seemed very fragile. To those who can recall the 1950's, the
relative security environment of Southeast Asia appears more assured today
than when the American involvement began; it will be at least difficult
for that generation of Americans, especially officials, to accept suddenly
that the U.S. involvement was not warranted. It was just this consideration that led Senator Fulbright and the Foreign Relations Committee to
deny Senate confirmation, as Assistant Secretary of State for East Asian
and Pacific Affairs, to Ambassador G. M. Godley. Senator Fulbright argued
that as Ambassador to Laos, and in other capacities, Mr. Godley was so
closely identified with the military-interventionist character of American
policy in East Asia in the postwar period that he would not perform effectively in what the Senator hoped would become a much different American
approach to the region in the 1970's.

In Tokyo, the ambivalence to which I have pointed derives from the
fact that Japan's long postwar pretense to be unconcerned with political
or security outcomes in Southeast Asia no longer convinces anyone. As a
Foreign Ministry spokesman said in early 1973, when discussing Japan's
willingness to provide materials to the Indochina cease-fire commission
(but somehow otherwise to stay uninvolved), 'The security of Asia is

connected directly with the security of Japan."[5]

That remark is worth noting not because it expressed a novel thought, but rather because it has been so long in coming, at least publicly. Analysts in Japan and elsewhere have recognized for years that Japan increasingly was developing a heavy stake in the economies of Southeast Asian countries, and was of course paying much attention to political developments as well. Based in part on the network of economic connections stemming from Japan's reparations program of the 1950's, Tokyo increasingly established itself during the 1960's as the dominant economic force in all countries of Southeast Asia -- with the exception only of North Vietnam. By 1970, Japan was the first trading partner of all these states, even supplanting the United States' historic position in the Philippines economy.

Nevertheless, it was common throughout the period in which Japan reached this ascendance -- primarily during the 1960's -- for Japanese leaders to argue that there was no necessary political derivative from their economic role in East Asia. Especially during the early years of the decade, for example, Japan carefully avoided associating with any of the regional efforts that were initiated or discussed, even though in every instance the main announced goal was Asian economic cooperation. By 1965-66, however, it began to be evident that Japan was concerned not to be left out altogether from Asian discussions concerned with "cooperation". In that period, Japan took the lead in establishing an important annual meeting of Ministers of Economic Development -- possibly to assure good information on development strategies but also no doubt to help exercise some influence through the leverage of its own investment and trade capabilities. When Japan took this step, her leaders were at pains to stress that the group had no political overtones, but so deeply-felt are Asian apprehensions about Japan's sheer size and economic might that these disclaimers were met with skepticism and frequently discounted.

In the same period (1966) Japan joined the Asian and Pacific Council (ASPAC). This action did seem something of a departure for Japan since ASPAC -- which was the product of South Korean initiatives -- had a clearly anti-communist and political coloration. Tokyo has always seemed un-

---

[5]Quoted in _Tokyo Shimbun_, 24 January 1973.

comfortable with the decision to join ASPAC, and may have done so in large part precisely because it was a Korean initiative. Indeed, critics have argued that the Japanese are apprehensive of too much independence when undertaken by their former possession, and in practice Tokyo has sought to prevent Seoul from gaining too much prestige and credit from the ASPAC venture. Japan's policies in the group have emphasized a desire to avoid the more blatantly political or "cold war" directions that it might be given under the influence of either Taiwan or South Korea, and in this effort they have generally been aided by some others -- notably Malaysia.

Yet the most pronounced sign that Japan might finally be prepared to shed its postwar "low posture" image in Asian international politics came in 1970 -- shortly after the American-South Vietnamese military intervention into Cambodia. That event was followed within weeks by a remarkable conference convened under Indonesian auspices in Djakarta. While the "Djakarta Conference" is hardly remembered today, it remains a landmark event. For not only was it the first time that smaller East Asian states attempted, without great-power instigation, to play a role in the overall security problems of the region, but it was marked by the fact that the Japanese also participated. All governments were represented either by their Prime Ministers or by their Foreign Ministers,[6] and the Japanese played a major role in an attempt to find some way by which to persuade all governments involved in the Cambodian hostilities to achieve a cease-fire. In fact, when the Conference decided to send a small delegation of senior representatives to Peking, Washington, and Moscow, the members of the delegation were the Deputy Foreign Ministers (or equivalent) from Indonesia, Malaysia, and Japan.[7]

That all-Asian initiative of 1970, designed to save Cambodia from the fate of the remainder of Indochina, obviously did not achieve its goal, and Japan soon stepped back into more familiar character by carefully avoiding having much to do with any side of the Cambodian conflict. The United States, for example, often sought to enlist Japan's participa-

---

[6]Only Singapore sent a lower level official.

[7]The high level of the mission is reflected in the fact that Japan's representative was Vice-Minister Hogen; Malaysia's representative was Ghazalie Schafie; and the representative of Indonesia was Anwar Seni, then Deputy to Foreign Minister Malik.

tion in 1970-72 (along with that of Australia and others) in efforts to provide economic and especially military assistance to the Cambodian government of Marshal Lon Nol. While this met with some success elsewhere (Australia, Malaysia, and Thailand each provided different levels of modest -- and often quite covert -- military assistance),[8] the Japanese steadfastly refused to contribute much more than medicines and other very limited assistance. It was argued that Japan had no business participating in such direct political matters, and of course frequent reference was made to Article Nine of the Constitution in order to reinforce the case that Japan could not legally undertake *any* military role or provide military assistance to anyone outside of the Japanese home islands.

It may have been these Japanese disclaimers of interest, and evident unwillingness to provide much more than bandages in the Indochina conflict, that led to its exclusion from the three-nation commission established by the United States and North Vietnam to oversee the Vietnam cease-fire they negotiated during 1972-73. It will be recalled that many nations throughout the world were mentioned as possible participants in the Commission, and that many reasons were given why some in Asia -- like India -- were not acceptable to one side or another. Yet no public evidence exists that efforts were made to recruit Japan's participation, and it has always seemed remarkable that aside from Indonesia, which clearly does have deep continuing interests in East Asian and Southeast Asian security matters, the other members of the Commission were such relatively unlikely participants as Canada and Hungary.

It was probably this circumstance precisely which led Japanese leaders, in the remarks mentioned at the outset of this discussion, to complain to the world that "nobody had sought" Tokyo's advice and involvement in the Indochina ceasefire arrangements. Indeed, Japan would seem to have been a nearly ideal member of the ceasefire commission -- particularly because it had avoided a close identification with American efforts in Vietnam and Cambodia and because through trade and other relationships, there are

---

[8]Conversations with senior military and civilian officials in Bangkok, Canberra, Kuala Lumpur, and other capitals, visited by the author during mid-1970 and mid-1971, indicated the nature of assistance that had been provided and was under discussion. Indeed, the Australian Government, which had prepared a list of "Types of Equipment produced [in Australia] which might be supplied to Vietnam" carried a handwritten addition: "Cambodia, etc.".

developing ties between Japan and North Vietnam. Yet despite these "objective" factors which favor greater Japanese roles in the region, and even if thinking in Tokyo had in fact developed by 1973 to the point where Japan would have been willing to participate in the ceasefire commission, it has nobody but itself to blame for its exclusion. For the Japanese have for so many years, and with such consistency, denied any possible involvement in Asian security matters that the world may be forgiven if it has taken these disclaimers seriously.

The question has to be asked whether this past behavior record, in which Japan has flirted with involvement but generally avoided even economic arrangements of a long-term nature[9], implies that Japan will hold to that posture. The question arises not primarily from an assumption that Japanese leaders objectively *desire* a greater "role" in Indochina, or to "dominate the region" as is sometimes suggested, but instead from a consideration of those international changes in Asia that point to less freedom for Japan to remain as aloof as she has been. The litany of those changes is familiar: the impact of American "disengagement"; greater Soviet initiatives in Asia -- as in Brezhnev's repeated calls for an Asian collective security system; and finally, of course, the now-undeniable evidence that Peking has divested itself of the ideological cloak that so weakened its Asian presence during the 1960's. Each of these factors, along with developments within Southeast Asia itself, pose questions to Japan for which the answers of the 1960's have a reduced relevance. Will Japan's policies and perspectives respond closely to these changes?

For the next several years it will be reasonable to project in Indochina and Southeast Asia a straight-line development of Japanese policy, tightly linked and very similar to the outlines of the policy in that region which Japan has established during the past half-dozen years. By this I mean a steady and perceptible increase in the visibility and presence of Japan in Southeast Asia, but accompanied always by major efforts in Tokyo and by Japanese representatives in the region to avoid the appearances of Japanese dominance. It needs to be remembered that Japan already is highly sensitive to apprehensions, most vocally expressed in Djakarta and Bangkok but increasingly found among almost all leading

---

[9]The exception is Tokyo's major investment in Indonesian oil.

Southeast Asians, of a recurrence of the "co-prosperity sphere" syndrome. Reflecting these considerations, Japan will seek to tie whatever policies it undertakes in Southeast Asia to already existing local initiatives, and for this purpose it will seek to make its approach conform with policies enunciated by the ASEAN nations.[10]

None of the Indochina states are members of ASEAN, however, and partly because the Japanese are very skeptical about a plethora of additional regional organizations, it can be expected that Tokyo will ultimately lend its support to an enlargement of ASEAN. Proposals for widening ASEAN have come from many quarters repeatedly since 1967; such disparate states as Ceylon and Australia, as well as Burma, Cambodia, and both Vietnams have been suggested for membership. Yet two factors have so far militated against additions. First, a state must be evidently "Southeast Asian" (an argument used by Indonesia and others to suggest gently that Australia would not be eligible); and second, direct involvement in the Indochina war has prevented membership of either of the Vietnams, Laos, or Cambodia. Indonesia, however, has long desired that at least Cambodia join, and Thai leaders believe that the door should be kept open to Rangoon (when and if Burma's relative hermit status should be alleviated). Indonesia and Thailand are probably agreed that South Vietnam is not likely to be acceptable unless North Vietnam also joins; there is good reason to believe that in the past Indonesian Foreign Minister Adam Malik has sought some form of "associate" or "observer" status in ASEAN for both Vietnams.

From Japan's perspective, such an enlargement of ASEAN will be quite acceptable, and probably very desirable. It was, after all, Japan's desire to encourage rational allocations of resources, including a pooling of investment information, that in 1966 led it to sponsor the Southeast Asian Ministerial Conference on Economic Development. In part because Japan increasingly is involved in the economies of all Southeast Asian nations, such agencies as the Ministry of International Trade and Investment and the Finance Ministry clearly intend to avoid duplicative and redundant development efforts, and it is reasonable also to assume that Tokyo has

---

[10]The Association of Southeast Asian Nations (ASEAN) was established in 1967 by Indonesia, Malaysia, Singapore, Philippines, and Thailand, but it has been clear from the outset that leadership in the body has come from Bangkok and Djakarta, and in recent years most strongly from the Indonesians.

not encouraged the "showcase" projects that often seemed to characterize the first development decade. Similar considerations led Japan to insist on an absolutely pre-eminent role in the Asian Development Bank; initially, in fact, Japan sought to locate the bank in Tokyo. When that effort was resisted the Japanese won a tacit understanding on all sides that the President of the Bank will in the foreseeable future remain a Japanese.

These efforts reflect a Japanese conviction that some form of coordination or "harmonization" is minimally desirable for stable economic development in Southeast Asia, and increasingly in recent years the Japanese have also concluded that the one organization most likely to be able to contribute to that goal is ASEAN. Tokyo's attitude towards ASEAN began to take shape several years ago, and by mid-1971 both the Finance Ministry and MITI had approved a plan by the Foreign Ministry to provide support to ASEAN of a "non-political", infrastructure nature.[11]

To the extent that Japan will now seek to encourage and to expand ASEAN, both in scope and significance, it is reasonable to expect that Japan will also work simultaneously for the dissolution of ASPAC. In part this will reflect an effort to emphasize Southeast Asian, as compared with Northeast Asian, matters, but it will also of course derive heavily from Japan's desire to relieve China's apprehensions of Japanese relationships with both Taiwan and South Korea. Ironically, however, it can be expected that Southeast Asian leaders will resist -- at least initially -- Japanese efforts to enlarge ASEAN, since almost any initiatives from Tokyo tend to be suspect within Southeast Asia. But Japan's efforts will also be regarded as likely to supplant the relatively more acceptable American involvement in the region -- and despite much of the rhetoric of the past decade from such capitals as Djakarta, Singapore, Kuala Lumpur, or Manila, it has to be recognized that a continued American presence is in fact widely desired among leaders there and elsewhere in Southeast Asia.

---

[11]In addition to earlier discussions (annually since 1962), this information derives from conversations at the *Gaimusho* in June-July 1971, at which officials asked this writer informally to test the receptiveness of Southeast Asian officials to direct Japanese assistance to ASEAN. Officials had in mind a supportive effort by which Japan would provide ASEAN headquarters in each capital with sophisticated information-processing equipment and other technical help, but not including, at least initially, direct Japanese financing of ASEAN development projects.

It can hardly be expected that a belated desire to retain an American "presence" will be successful; any more than it can be imagined that the present leaders of the ASEAN states will in fact resist genuine possibilities to enlarge the body by adding the Indochina states -- even if the suggestion does come now from Tokyo. In part this will be because these same leaders have argued for years that the Indochina states should be involved in any Southeast Asian regional framework, and also because the Japanese will make offers of region-wide assistance too good to be refused.

With these opportunities for help, however, will also come realities of Japanese political involvement that will in some cases add to tension among Southeast Asian states; for example, if Japan lends its support to the proposal for "neutralization" of the region, advocated by Malaysia but looked upon with much suspicion by Indonesia, Singapore, and perhaps others. Similarly, Japan's desire to retain unrestricted transit rights in the Straits of Malacca will run counter -- at least initially -- to strongly-held convictions in Indonesia and to a lesser extent in Malaysia. Indeed, the opportunities for severe disagreements on this subject are major, since the United States has also expressed its view that the Malacca Straits should continue to be regarded as an international waterway.

While it appears reasonable to project a relatively stable development of Japanese policy in Southeast Asia and Indochina, in which the nature and scale of Japan's presence will grow perceptibly to include some form of political involvement by the end of the decade, the nature of the American presence seems much less likely to proceed along such a straight-line projection. In contrast to Japan, where there conflicting voices that argue alternative policies towards Indochina and Southeast Asia, there seems in the United States to be a veritable chasm separating the contrasting policies and their advocates.

One position, of course, will be characterized by very strong arguments that press for withdrawal from all political and security involvement in the entire Southeast Asian region. Among other considerations, this position will stress "multipolarity". Proponents will make the point that even if a unilateral American presence was required in Southeast Asia two decades ago, the long-standing American concern to avoid dominance in Asia by any single great power is now automatically assured by major external factors. Among these are the resurgence of China and its enmity towards

a Soviet Union that is itself increasingly concerned with East Asia, and
the "inevitable" need for Japan (as a result of its apprehensions towards
both Peking and Moscow) also to become involved in the region. The resulting likelihood that the U.S.S.R., China, and Japan will therefore contest for some presence in the Southeast Asia and Indochina region will, in
other words, be pointed to as sufficient reason for the United States now
to disengage fully from its solitary policeman's role.

Yet there are important arguments on the other side, which can make
a strong case for a continued and important presence by the United States.
While there is no denying that Americans have tired of Vietnam, it remains
a fact that the United States has invested colossal resources and energies
toward the continued existence of some sort of South Vietnam -- at least
for the duration of time sometimes referred to as a "decent interval".
This is the argument which stresses that American credibility is involved
in the ultimate future of South Vietnam. While there may be few Americans
who will press this to the point of requiring a direct and continuing presence in Vietnam, it will be stressed that American credibility, which is
involved in global regions in addition to Southeast Asia, requires a continued presence at least in Thailand.[12]

The Thai relationship is buttressed by a bilateral American commitment that grows out of but is partly separate from SEATO. The Thai relationship, in other words, can reasonably be regarded by and portrayed to
Americans as a formal and binding commitment -- and among a people who have
always been receptive to the view that treaties and other solemn commit-
ments should be honored, it does not yet seem prudent to dismiss the sense
of obligation implied by the Rusk-Thanat agreement of 1962. While this
consideration may be subject to criticism as simply another "legalism" that
ought not to deflect the course of American foreign policy from its more
"basic" national interests, the record of American foreign policy behavior
contains impressive evidence that such legalisms have great weight.

---

[12]The point has often been made that President Nixon, among others,
did not wish to become identified with a cease-fire arrangement for Indochina that would quickly turn sour, in apprehension of later charges (remi-
niscent of those that were leveled at Democrats in the 1950's with regard
to China) that his administration had "lost" Indochina. He was, after all,
among those who spearheaded those charges against President Truman.

Similar considerations apply to the Philippines, where a combination
of long historical associations, as well as very formal bilateral and multilateral (SEATO) arrangements, can still be cited in support of direct American support for the Manila government. While there has been considerable
attention in the American press and intellectual community to the recent
record of Philippines' President Marcos in severely curtailing most sem-
blances of civil liberties and political democracy, there are very few
indications that either the United States government or other leaders have
sought to establish greater "distance" between Washington and the auto-
cratic behavior of President Marcos. Indeed, it is likely instead that
official Americans, as well as those with long-standing economic relationships with the Philippines, may quietly welcome the greater degree of
order which Marcos has apparently achieved, and the energy with which his
government has sought to deal with its long-standing problem of low-level
banditry and insurgency.[13]

Finally, it has to be recognized that in addition to these strategic
and political considerations that apply to various parts of Southeast Asia,
a case can increasingly be made for an American dependence upon economic
resources within the region. At present this applies most dramatically to
Indonesia, whose low-sulphur oil in particular has become an outstandingly
important investment and exploration attraction for Americans (as well as
Japanese). Ever since the consolidation of President Suharto's power in
Indonesia in 1966-67, and the concomitant adoption of an investment law
and development plans acceptable to Western states, there has been a dra-
matic reversion to the old notion of Indonesia as a fabulously well-endowed
storehouse of mineral resources. Partly through the efforts of the IGGI
(an international, Netherlands-based consortium of donors and creditors
established to monitor and coordinate Indonesian development plans), there
has been both major economic progress in Indonesia and major American investment in those Indonesian resources which even now are recognized as
scarce and extremely valuable to the American economy. Oil is only the

---

[13]For comment on this point, *see* the discussion in the Christian
Science Monitor of 21 September 1973. Reports indicate that foreign investment has begun to increase, and that business conditions, at least,
are significantly improved since mid-1972 when Marcos declared martial
law.

most prominent of these at present, and because continued access to these resources is seen to depend on a continuation of Indonesia's security and stability, it will not be surprising to hear increasing arguments on the desirability of an American presence in or near Indonesian territory.

Any one of these arguments for a continued American presence in Southeast Asia, however -- whether they derive from older historical ties, recent military involvements, or alleged future economic relationships of dependence -- will run counter to long-standing American attitudes. The heart of the problem is that the United States has regarded Southeast Asia, and Indochina, as important to American security interests only in *instrumental* and indirect terms, rather than as a region of intrinsic importance to the United States. Initially, for example, the United States gave importance to Southeast Asia because it was believed that the U.S. was engaged in a conflict with global ideological connotations. In that era, to "lose" any state to Communist control was seen, in traditional zero-sum-game terms, as a negative outcome. Similarly, American security objectives in Southeast Asia were partially conceptualized in the light of American interests in the security of Japan, and probably Australia as well. It was believed, in other words, that to the extent that those relatively major states were dependent on the continued stability and security of the Southeast Asia region, but were unable themselves to provide for that security, an indirect United States interest was justifiable.

Today, however, no such weakness can be argued for Japan, and many considerations which previously seemed to place Australian security in doubt (including the possibility of Japanese ambitions regarding Australia) have greatly altered or disappeared. Similarly, as the extent of Sino-Soviet rivalries and fears have become undeniably clear, it has also become evident that the United States no longer faces the same sort of "ideological" struggle which was previously perceived. At the very minimum, it is clear that the United States no longer faces a prospect of Sino-Soviet close cooperation or collusion, to say nothing of the alliance or "bloc" that was regarded as a real threat to security in East Asia and Southeast Asia during the 1950's.

It is of course ironical that the most compelling arguments for American disengagement come precisely at that point in time when the United States might indeed find that it has intrinsic, especially economic, interests in Southeast Asia. But putting that potential difficulty aside, the broader considerations would seem to argue for an American position of considerable relaxation towards the security problems of Southeast Asia during the 1970's -- if the region's traditional role of only "instrumental" importance is sustained.

One consequence is that those American policy-makers who have matured in the tradition that the United States does have a need to retain an important security presence in Southeast Asia, and who refuse to accept that the twenty-year involvement in Indochina can now be allowed to be swept away as if the investment were for nothing, will therefore face the major problem of persuading a tired public that a continued presence and possibility of reinvolvement is justified. It may be that they will be able to generate support by pointing to American needs for Indonesia's "sweet" oil, or to other tangible considerations, but this seems doubtful. Instead, as Robert W. Tucker has recently and elaborately reminded us, American security policies in the past have had to draw for support upon some grander sense of mission and purpose.[14]

For the United States, at least, there are no evident signs of what such larger "purpose" might be, and most leading Americans (and many Japanese) tend to shudder at the prospect that Japan might again develop a grand sense of mission in the Pacific. With regard to the United States, moreover, it is a major question whether Americans will have the will to continue to play a security role in Southeast Asia, whatever the purposes that might now be identified. And even more uncertain is whether the economy of the United States -- whatever the will of its people -- can sustain a credible role of significance in the security problems of Southeast Asia.

---

[14]*See* his chapter, "The American Outlook: Change and Continuity", in Robert E. Osgood, *et al.*, <u>Retreat from Empire: The First Nixon Administration</u>, Volume II in <u>American and the World</u> (Baltimore: The Johns Hopkins University Press, 1973), pp. 29-78.

Publ. No. 1 - THE NEW ENGLISH OF THE ONITSHA CHAPBOOKS. By Harold
Reeves Collins. Pp. v, 17. 1968. $1.50

Publ. No. 2 - DIRECTIONS IN GHANAIAN LINGUISTICS: A Brief Survey.
By Paul F. A. Kotey. Pp. v, 15. 1969. $1.50

Publ. No. 3 - DEFINING NATIONAL PURPOSE IN LESOTHO. By Richard F.
Weisfelder. Pp. xi, 28. 1969. $2.00

Publ. No. 4 - RECENT AGRICULTURAL CHANGE EAST OF MOUNT KENYA. By
Frank E. Bernard. Pp. v, 36. 1969. $2.50

Publ. No. 5 - THE STRUGGLE AGAINST SLEEPING SICKNESS IN NYASALAND AND
NORTHERN RHODESIA, 1900-1922. By Norman H. Pollock.
Pp. v, 16. 1969. $1.50

Publ. No. 6 - BOTSWANA AND ITS SOUTHERN NEIGHBOR: The Patterns of
Linkage and the Options in Statecraft. By Richard Dale.
Pp. vii, 22. 1970. $1.75

Publ. No. 7 - WOLF COURTS GIRL: The Equivalence of Hunting and Mating
in Bushman Thought. By Daniel F. McCall. Pp. v, 19.
1970. $1.50

Publ. No. 8 - MARKERS IN ENGLISH-INFLUENCED SWAHILI CONVERSATION. By
Carol M. Eastman. Pp. v, 20. 1970. $1.75

Publ. No. 9 - THE TERRITORIAL EXPANSION OF THE NANDI OF KENYA, 1500-
1905. By Bob J. Walter. Pp. vii, 30. 1970. $2.50

Publ. No. 10- SOME GEOGRAPHICAL ASPECTS OF WEST AFRICAN DEVELOPMENT.
By R. J. Harrison Church. Pp. v, 29. 1970. $2.50

Publ. No. 11- THE IMPACT OF THE PROTEGE SYSTEM IN MOROCCO, 1880-1912.
By Leland Bowie. Pp. vi, 16. 1970. $1.50

Publ. No. 12- MARKET DEVELOPMENT IN TRADITIONALLY MARKETLESS SOCIETIES:
A Perspective on East Africa. By Charles M. Good.
Pp. vi, 34. 1971. $2.25

Publ. No. 13- SOUTH AFRICA'S OUTWARD STRATEGY: A Foreign Policy Dilemma
for the United States. By Larry W. Bowman. Pp. vii, 25.
1971. $2.00

Publ. No. 14- BANTU EDUCATION AND THE EDUCATION OF AFRICANS IN SOUTH
AFRICA. By R. Hunt Davis, Jr. Pp. vii, 53. 1972.
$3.00

Publ. No. 15- TOWARD A THEORY OF THE AFRICAN UPPER STRATUM IN SOUTH
AFRICA. By Thomas E. Nyquist. Pp. vii, 56. 1972.
$3.00

Publ. No. 16- THE BASOTHO MONARCHY: A Spent Force or a Dynamic Political
Factor? By Richard F. Weisfelder. Pp. ix, 97. 1972.
$3.50

Publ. No. 17- YORUBA PROVERBS: Translation and Annotation. By Bernth
Lindfors and Oyekan Owomoyela. Pp. ix, 82. 1973. $3.25

Publ. No. 18- POST-MILITARY COUP STRATEGY IN UGANDA: Amin's Early Attempts
to Consolidate Political Support. By Jeffrey T. Strate.
Pp. vii, 70. 1973. $3.25

Publ. No. 19- HIGHLAND MOSAIC: A Critical Anthology of Ethiopian Litera-
ture in English. Compiled by Paul E. Huntsberger. Pp. ix,
122. 1973. $4.25

Publ. No. 20- THE KENYA NATIONAL YOUTH SERVICE: A Governmental Response
to Young Political Activists. By Richard L. Coe. Pp. vi,
33. 1973. $2.25

Publ. No. 21- CONSTRAINTS ON THE EXPANSION OF COMMERCIAL AGRICULTURE:
Iringa District, Tanzania. By Marilyn Silberfein. Pp. vii,
51. 1974. $3.00

Publ. No. 22- ECHO AND CHORUSES: "Ballad of the Cells" and Selected
Shorter Poems. By Cosmo Pieterse. Pp. ix, 66. 1974.
$3.25

ALSO: WEST/AFRICAN PIDGIN-ENGLISH: A Descriptive Linguistic Analysis
with Texts and Glossary from the Cameroon Area. By Gilbert D.
Schneider. Pp. xiv, 242. 1969. $6.00

This book is an attempt to apply the basic principles of structural
linguistics to West African Pidgin-English. After an introductory
chapter which deals with the general characteristics of the language
as spoken in the Cameroon area, the author proceeds to the treatment of sounds, meaningful units, and sentence patterns. A glossary
and bibliography are included.

SOUTHEAST ASIA PROGRAM
CENTER FOR INTERNATIONAL STUDIES
OHIO UNIVERSITY
ATHENS, OHIO 45701

Publ. No. 1 - TREASURES AND TRIVIA: Doctoral Dissertations on Southeast Asia Accepted by Universities in the United States. Compiled by Lian The and Paul W. van der Veur. Pp. xiv, 141, Appendix, Index. 1968. $4.50

Publ. No. 2 - PUBLIC PROTEST IN INDONESIA. By Ann Ruth Willner. Pp. vii, 14. 1968. $1.50

Publ. No. 3 - DEVELOPMENTAL CHALLENGE IN MALAYSIA. By Siew Nim Chee. Pp. v, 17. 1968. $1.50

Publ. No. 4 - THE USE OF HISTORY. By Wang Gungwu. Pp. vii, 17. 1968. $1.50

Publ. No. 5 - THE TRADITIONAL USE OF THE FORESTS IN MAINLAND SOUTHEAST ASIA. Bu James L. Cobban. Out of print.

Publ. No. 6 - CONFLICT AND POLITICAL DEVELOPMENT IN SOUTHEAST ASIA: An Exploration in the International Implications of Comparative Theory. By Gerald S. Maryanov. Out of print.

Publ. No. 7 - SRI PADUKA: The Exile of the Prince of Ayodhya. Translated by S. M. Ponniah. Out of print.

Publ. No. 8 - AGRARIAN UNREST IN THE PHILIPPINES: Guardia de Honor -- Revitalization within the Revolution; Rizalistas -- Contemporary Revitalization Movements in the Philippines. By David R. Sturtevant. Pp. vii, 30. 1969. $2.24

Publ. No. 9 - PANDANGGO-SA-ILAW: The Politics of Occidental Mindoro. By Remigio E. Agpalo. Pp. ix, 23. 1969. $1.75

Publ. No. 10- REPRESSION AND REVOLT: The Origins of the 1948 Communist Insurrection in Malaya and Singapore. By Michael R. Stenson. Out of print.

Publ. No. 11- RUBBER AND THE MALAYSIAN ECONOMY: Implications of Declining Prices. By Tan Sri Lim Swee Aun. Pp. v, 31. 1969. $2.25

Publ. No. 12- EDUCATION AND SOCIAL CHANGE IN COLONIAL INDONESIA: I. Progress and Procrastination in Education in Indonesia prior to World War II; II. The Social and Geographical Origins of Dutch-Educated Indonesians. By Paul W. van der Veur. Pp. xiii, 49. 1969. $2.75

Publ. No. 13- COMMUNAL VIOLENCE IN MALAYSIA 1969: The Political Aftermath. By Felix V. Gagliano. Out of print.

Publ. No. 14- SOVIET AND AMERICAN AID TO INDONESIA 1949-1968. By Usha Mahajani. Pp. vii, 42. 1970. $2.75

Publ. No. 15- POLITICS AMONG BURMANS: A Study of Intermediary Leaders. By John Badgley. Pp. x, 115. 1970. $4.00

Publ. No. 16- TRADE AND EMPIRE IN MALAYA AND SINGAPORE, 1869-1874. By D. R. SarDesai. Pp. v, 17. 1970. $1.50

Publ. No. 17- THE EXPANSION OF THE VIETNAM WAR INTO CAMBODIA: Action and Response by the Governments of North Vietnam, South Vietnam, Cambodia, and the United States. By Peter A. Poole. Pp. xi, 59. 1970. $3.00

Publ. No. 18- THE PRE-WORLD WAR II PERANAKAN CHINESE PRESS OF JAVA: A Preliminary Survey. By Leo Suryadinata. Pp. ix, 35. 1971. $2.50

Publ. No. 19- A REVIEW OF COMMUNITY-ORIENTED ECOLOGICAL RESEARCH IN THE PHILIPPINES. By Robert A. Bullington. Pp. ix, 31. 1971. $2.25

Publ. No. 20- A BIBLIOGRAPHY OF PHILIPPINE LINGUISTICS. By Nobleza C. Asuncion-Landé. Pp. xxi, 146, Index. 1971. $4.50

Publ. No. 21- THE BURMA-YUNNAN RAILWAY: Anglo-French Rivalry in Mainland Southeast Asia and South China, 1895-1902. By J. Chandran. Pp. ix, 110. 1971. $4.00

Publ. No. 22- THE NORTH BORNEO CHARTERED COMPANY'S ADMINISTRATION OF THE BAJAU, 1878-1909: The Pacification of a Maritime, Nomadic People. By James F. Warren. Out of print.

Publ. No. 23- PROMINENT INDONESIAN CHINESE IN THE TWENTIETH CENTURY: A Preliminary Survey. By Leo Suryadinata. Out of print.

Publ. No. 24- PEACOCKS, PAGODAS, AND PROFESSOR HALL: A Critique of the Persisting Use of Historiography as an Apology for British Empire-Building in Burma. By Manuel Sarkisyanz. Pp. xi, 57. 1972. $3.00

Publ. No. 25- IMBALANCES IN DEVELOPMENT: The Indonesian Experience. By Selo Soemardjan. Pp. v, 21. 1972. $1.75

Publ. No. 26- THE VERHANDELINGEN VAN HET BATAVIAASCH GENOOTSCHAP: An Annotated Content Analysis. Compiled by Lian The and Paul W. van der Veur. Pp. xi, 140, Index. 1973. $4.50

Publ. No. 27- JAPAN'S SCHEME FOR THE LIBERATION OF BURMA: The Role of the Minami Kikan and the "Thirty Comrades". By Won Z. Yoon. Pp. xi, 54, Bibliography. 1973. $3.00

Publ. No. 28- EDUCATIONAL SPONSORSHIP BY ETHNICITY: A Preliminary Analysis of the West Malaysian Experience. By Yoshimitsu Takei, John C. Bock, and Bruce Saunders. Pp. vii, 37. 1973. $2.75

Publ. No. 29- BLOOD, BELIEVER, AND BROTHER: The Development of Voluntary Associations in Malaysia. By Stephen A. Douglas and Paul Pedersen. Pp. viii, 111, Appendix. 1973. $4.00

Publ. No. 30- THE DYNAMICS OF POLITICS AND ADMINISTRATION IN RURAL THAILAND. By Clark D. Neher. Pp. ix, 94. 1974. $3.75

Publ. No. 31- PEASANT CITIZENS: Politics, Religion, and Modernization in Kelantan, Malaysia. By Manning Nash. Pp. xi, 170, Bibliography. 1974. $5.00

Publ. No. 32- MARGINAL MAN IN A COLONIAL SOCIETY: A Discussion of Salah Asuhan by Abdoel Moeis. By David de Queljoe. Pp. v, 38. 1974. $2.75

Publ. No. 33- THE NEUTRALIZATION OF SOUTHEAST ASIA: An Analysis of the Malaysian/ASEAN Proposal. By Marvin C. Ott. Pp. vii, 50. 1974. $3.00

Publ. No. 34- THE LAND-TO-THE-TILLER PROGRAM AND RURAL RESOURCE MOBILIZATION IN THE MEKONG DELTA OF SOUTH VIETNAM. By C. Stuart Callison. Pp. vii, 41. 1974. $2.75

Publ. No. 35- THE FUTURE OF BURMA IN PERSPECTIVE: A Symposium. Edited and with an Introduction by Josef Silverstein. Pp. xii, 92. 1974. $4.00

Publ. No. 36- INDOCHINA: PERSPECTIVES FOR RECONCILIATION. Edited and with an introduction by Peter A. Poole. Pp. vii, 84. 1975. $4.00

ALSO DISTRIBUTOR OF:

INTERNATIONAL BIOGRAPHICAL DIRECTORY OF SOUTHEAST ASIA SPECIALISTS. Compiled by Robert O. Tilman. Pp. xxxv, 337. 1969. Special price: $1.25

A collection of about 1,000 vitae of Southeast Asia specialists throughout the world preceded by an introductory analysis of the data collected. The study was undertaken as a project by the Inter-University Southeast Asia Committee of the Association for Asian Studies.

L2